THE LAW AND THE PROMISE

A PRONOMIAN
POCKET GUIDE TO
GALATIANS 3-4

JONATHAN A. BROWN

The Law and the Promise: A Pronomian Pocket Guide to Galatians 3–4

Copyright © 2025 Jonathan A. Brown. All rights reserved.

Pronomian Publishing LLC
Clover, SC 29710

ISBN: 979-8-9908630-5-7

Publisher grants permission to reference short quotations (fewer than 300 words) in reviews, magazines, newspapers, websites, or other publications. Request for permission to reproduce more than 300 words can be made at **www.pronomianpublishing.com/contact**

Scripture quotations taken from the (NASB®) New American Standard Bible®, Copyright © 1960, 1971, 1977, 1995, 2020 by The Lockman Foundation. Used by permission. All rights reserved. lockman.org.

In *The Law and the Promise*, Jonathan Brown delivers a powerful and much needed corrective to centuries of tradition that have misread Paul's intent in Galatians. Drawing on a rigorous exegetical approach, the author dismantles the notion that "under the law" equates to Torah observance. Instead, this work persuasively argues that Paul's concern was not the abrogation of God's holy, righteous, and good Torah but its misuse as a means of justification. The careful analysis of the Law's role as guardian, revealer of sin, and guide for sanctification demonstrates conclusively that the Torah and the Promise are not a contradiction but two harmonious, distinct, and integral components of God's unified redemptive plan. This book is an essential read for any serious student of Scripture seeking to understand the biblical balance of freedom and responsibility in Messiah.
—Matthew Nappier, Ph.D.

I have long said that one of the most misunderstood writers of Scripture is the apostle Paul. This is especially true when it comes to Paul's statements about the Law, which at times seem to contradict each other. In *The Law and the Promise*, Jonathan Brown helps us to move closer to understanding Paul and making sense of his teachings about the Law in Galatians 3 and 4 by examining them in their first-century Jewish context. You may or may not agree with every point made, but this book is a needed addition to our understanding of Paul and his thinking about the Law—and it will make you question and reconsider previous assumptions you may have held, as all good books should.
—Mike Davis, Th.D.

Jonathan's book on Galatians is full of wisdom and insight, coming from his rigorous study of the book, drawing out the richness of Paul's

letter in fresh and meaningful ways. His careful attention to the history and culture behind the text makes the message come alive. This work is thoughtful, scholarly, and encouraging, and I believe anyone who reads it will be deeply blessed and challenged by it.
—Heather Quiroz

CONTENTS

Introduction 1

1. Setting the Stage 7
2. The Harmony of the Word 21
3. Under What, Exactly? 27
4. Guardians and Managers 37
5. Back to Basics 45
6. A Completely Separate Purpose 53

Appendix A(pologetics) 67

Postscript 83

Bibliography 85

INTRODUCTION

Paul's letter to the Galatians is one of the most influential letters in all the New Testament. Rightly so, as so many of the topics Paul addresses in it remain relevant to all believers in all times and places. Themes abound in the letter: grace, charity, love, covenant. The letter contains a range of impactful passages, from one of the most resounding statements about equality in the ancient world (Gal. 3:28) to the fruit of the Spirit (Gal. 5:22–23). Throughout Church history, the letter has been variously interpreted and applied. Augustine, one of the most influential and prolific writers in Christian history, wrote only one complete commentary on an entire book of the Bible, and that happens to be Galatians.[1] A millennium later, Martin Luther expended more effort on writing and revising his work on Galatians than any other, and considered it the most important of his works.[2]

Galatians has arguably shaped Christian theology more than any other book of the New Testament (though Romans could also reasonably vie for first place). This letter has left an indelible mark on Church

---

1   Gerald Bray, "Review of Augustine's Commentary on Galatians: Introduction, Text, Translation and Notes by Eric Plumer," *The Churchman* 118, no. 1–4 (2004), 380.

2   Joseph Barber Lightfoot, ed., *St. Paul's Epistle to the Galatians. A Revised Text with Introduction, Notes, and Dissertations*, 4th ed., Classic Commentaries on the Greek New Testament (London: Macmillan and Co., 1874), 68.

doctrines, especially in its treatment of faith, freedom, and the Law. But why, then, does Galatians continue to spark such intense debate, particularly on the question of Torah observance? For centuries, most Christian teaching has interpreted Galatians as an emphatic rejection of the Torah's authority for believers, with Paul seen as proclaiming that followers of Christ are no longer bound to follow the Law's commands. Kenneth Boles' commentary on Galatians offers a succinct summary of this position in just a single paragraph:

> This epistle is our charter of Christian freedom, our declaration of independence from slavery to the law. Throughout the history of the church the message of Galatians has been needed to free men from chains of false doctrine. When the early Judaizers tried to bind men to the old commandments from Sinai, Galatians set them free. When the apostate church of the Dark Ages tried to bind men to a papal system of salvation by penance and works, Galatians set them free. When modern legalists try to bind us to a joyless religion of superior "rightness," Galatians sets us free.[3]

At the center of these claims lies what, on the surface, seems to be a straightforward teaching from the apostle: in Galatians 3:19–29, Paul proclaims that the Law was "added," that the Law was our guardian (or "tutor" as some translations render it), and that, now that faith has come through Messiah, we no longer need that guardian. So engrained in tradition and translation is it, that this seems like the only way to read the passage. Here is the passage in question:

---

3   Kenneth L. Boles, *Galatians & Ephesians*, The College Press NIV Commentary (Joplin, MO: College Press, 1993), 13.

Introduction

> Why the Law then? It was added on account of the violations, having been ordered through angels at the hand of a mediator, until the Seed would come to whom the promise had been made. Now a mediator is not for one party only; but God is only one. Is the Law then contrary to the promises of God? Far from it! For if a law had been given that was able to impart life, then righteousness would indeed have been based on law. But the Scripture has confined everyone under sin, so that the promise by faith in Jesus Christ might be given to those who believe. But before faith came, we were kept in custody under the Law, being confined for the faith that was destined to be revealed. Therefore the Law has become our guardian to lead us to Christ, so that we may be justified by faith. But now that faith has come, we are no longer under a guardian. For you are all sons and daughters of God through faith in Christ Jesus. For all of you who were baptized into Christ have clothed yourselves with Christ. There is neither Jew nor Greek, there is neither slave nor free, there is neither male nor female; for you are all one in Christ Jesus. And if you belong to Christ, then you are Abraham's descendants, heirs according to promise.
> —Galatians 3:19–29

The near consensus regarding the traditional interpretation has been bolstered by centuries of tradition and teaching within the Church that consistently stresses Paul's emphasis on grace over—and opposed to—law, and freedom over obligation. Yet, as more scholars revisit Paul's message, questions arise: Could we have misunderstood Paul's view of the Torah in Galatians? Was his teaching more nuanced than traditionally thought? Has the widely accepted reading of Galatians, after nearly 2,000 years of interpretation, overlooked crucial aspects of Paul's approach to the Torah? I find these questions not merely worth considering, but indeed an imperative for the believer today to consider. I contend that this letter still has more to reveal about the relationship between faith and law and about the balance of freedom and responsibility in the life of a believer. It is my goal in the present work to show that the traditional view is in need of some corrective actions. In this work, I will argue that it is necessary to reexamine the apostle's teachings regarding the Law in Galatians because it must be harmonized with the rest of Scripture. Additionally, I will argue that the evidence does not lend itself to the abrogation of the Law based on Galatians 3, but merely points to a certain use or function that it once held, and that the very assertion of "law *or* grace" is itself a false dichotomy. That is, ultimately, we will answer the question: is the Law contrary to the Promise? The outline below shows how we will walk through this topic logically in this brief work:

- Chapter 1: Background on why the traditional approach to Paul's teaching on the Torah cannot be sustained considering the growing biblical and theological evidence.
- Chapter 2: The Historical and Cultural Context of Galatians—Exploring the specific circumstances and setting that prompted Paul's letter.
- Chapter 3: Beyond "Under the Law"—Demonstrating that Paul's phrase does not imply believers should reject Torah observance and clarifying that Torah itself was never the source of bondage to sin.
- Chapter 4: The Nurturing Path to Maturity—Analyzing Paul's use of "pedagogue," "guardian," and "manager" as beneficial guides rather than harsh taskmasters, illustrating their positive role in spiritual development.

- Chapter 5: Covenant Continuity in Genesis—Examining how Paul's understanding of Torah covenantal texts shaped his "Sarah vs. Hagar" allegory in Galatians, revealing deeper connections to his overall theological framework.
- Chapter 6: The Complementary Purpose of Torah—Establishing that the Torah works alongside rather than against the promise, serving a distinct yet harmonious function in God's redemptive plan.

As a supplementary work, I have included a short appendix as well to address a few specific arguments that scholars and other interpreters raise against the notion for which I am advocating in this book. While not exhaustive, I hope it helps to anticipate and adequately answer some of the questions that the reader will develop while working through the present volume. I also hope it offers a little critical engagement with the "other side" without distracting from the work as a whole.

For my own part, I have spent significant time working and wading through Paul's letter to the Galatians. While working on my Master's in Biblical Languages at Liberty University, I wrote an essay that would eventually become largely the thesis of this book, centered on exegeting the passages in question from Galatians 3. I wrote that essay for a Galatians Exegesis course, which requires having already passed multiple successive courses in Biblical Greek. I also taught a multi-part series going through Galatians section by section during my tenure as Messianic Pastor at Nehemiah Restoration Fellowship in Tennessee, from 2021–2022. I say this only to assert that my work on Galatians is not an afterthought, but rather is the fruit of many years laboring—in love—in this wonderful, blessed Scripture written by the apostle to the Gentiles.

Introduction

As an aside, throughout this work I will consistently refer to Jesus by his Hebrew (Jewish) name, Yeshua (aside from direct quotes from other sources). This is in keeping with my own personal practice as well as the practice and preference of my local faith community. This is not a point of pet doctrine or dogma but is my habit and practice.

Lastly, I hope and pray this work blesses you, the reader, and guides you further on your journey to discovering the light, life, and beauty of the Law of God.

CHAPTER 1
SETTING THE STAGE

Paul's epistle to the Galatians is often referred to as the "Magna Carta of Christian liberty."[1] For centuries, it has been a touchstone for discussions about law, grace, faith, and salvation. Martin Luther, whose theological insights sparked the Protestant Reformation, considered Galatians his favorite letter, calling it "my own epistle, to which I have plighted my troth... it is my Katie von Bora."[2] The theological impact of this relatively brief letter cannot be overstated. Yet despite its profound influence, Galatians remains one of the most misunderstood letters in the New Testament, particularly regarding its teachings about Torah observance. Before delving into the text itself, it is essential to establish the historical, cultural, and sociological context in which this letter was written. Understanding the background will help us to avoid common interpretive pitfalls and grasp Paul's intended message more accurately.

The Region of Galatia: North or South?

One of the first questions we must address concerns the identity of the letter's recipients. The region known as "Galatia" in the first century CE could refer to two different geographical areas within what is now modern Turkey. This has led to what scholars call the

---

1   Philip Graham Ryken, *Galatians*, Reformed Expository Commentary, ed. Richard D. Phillips, Philip Graham Ryken, and Daniel M. Doriani (Phillipsburg, NJ: P&R Publishing, 2005), 216.

2   Richard N. Longenecker, *Galatians*, vol. 41, Word Biblical Commentary (Dallas: Word, Incorporated, 1990), liii.

"North Galatian" and "South Galatian" theories regarding the identity of Paul's audience.[3]

North Galatia was an ethnographic region in the central highlands of Asia Minor, inhabited by Celtic tribes (called "Gauls" by Romans, hence "Galatia") who had migrated there from Europe in the third century BCE. This area eventually became the Roman province of Galatia but represented its more northern regions.

South Galatia refers to the southern portion of the Roman province, which included cities like Antioch of Pisidia, Iconium, Lystra, and Derbe—cities that Paul is explicitly recorded as having visited during his first missionary journey in Acts 13–14. These cities were not ethnically Galatian but fell under Rome's provincial administration of Galatia.

The question of whether Paul was addressing believers in North or South Galatia may not seem to matter on the surface, but it significantly impacts our understanding of the letter's dating and context. If he was writing to North Galatia, the letter would have been written later in his ministry (around 55–57 CE), after the events described in Acts 18. If he was writing to South Galatia, the letter could have been composed much earlier, possibly around 48–49 CE, making it potentially Paul's earliest preserved epistle.[4] The evidence internal to the letter itself also lends to this, as "Galatians" could refer only to a specific ethnic group (as Paul uses the word to address the readers in Gal. 3:1). If he wrote only to this small group of Celts, however, then his readership would be very small and isolated. More likely, he refers

---

[3] Craig S. Keener, *Galatians: A Commentary* (Grand Rapids, MI: Baker Academic: A Division of Baker Publishing Group, 2019), 16–17.
[4] Keener, Galatians, 17.

to them as "Galatians" either to encompass the entirety of the Galatian region, or in reference to the entire "congregation" of Galatia.

While scholars continue to debate this question, the evidence increasingly favors the South Galatian theory for several reasons:

1. Acts does not explicitly mention Paul visiting North Galatian cities, but his work in South Galatian cities is well-documented.
2. The issues addressed in Galatians align closely with the controversy described in Acts 15 regarding Gentile inclusion in the community of believers, which would place the letter around the time of the Jerusalem Council.
3. In Galatians 4:13, Paul mentions having preached to the Galatians "the first time" (implying at least a second visit), which corresponds with his first and second missionary journeys through South Galatia as recorded in Acts.
4. The presence of Barnabas in the narrative (Gal. 2:1, 9, 13) suggests the letter was written when Barnabas was still Paul's traveling companion, which was true during the first missionary journey but not later journeys.[5]

If we accept the South Galatian theory, as I believe the evidence warrants, this would place the writing of Galatians at a pivotal moment in the early Yeshua movement—a time when foundational questions about Gentile inclusion and the relationship between faith in Messiah and Torah observance were being actively debated.

---

5   Grant R. Osborne, *Galatians: Verse by Verse*, Osborne New Testament Commentaries (Bellingham, WA: Lexham Press, 2017), 4–5.

The Imperial Context: Living Under Rome

To fully appreciate the situation facing the Galatian believers, we must understand the political realities of living under Roman imperial rule in the first century. The Roman Empire maintained its vast territories through a combination of military presence, administrative control, and cultural assimilation. A key element of Roman governance was the Imperial Cult—the state-sponsored worship of the emperor and Roma (the deified personification of Rome). The Imperial Cult was a means of combining socio-political existence with religious life.[6] Participation in the Imperial Cult was considered a civic duty for all inhabitants of the empire. Citizens and subjects were expected to offer sacrifices, burn incense, and participate in festivals honoring the emperor and Roman deities. This was not merely a religious requirement but a political one—a public demonstration of loyalty to Rome.[7]

For most inhabitants of the empire in the first century, this presented no significant moral dilemma. The polytheistic religious systems prevalent throughout the Mediterranean world could easily accommodate additional deities, including a deified emperor (Caesar). However, for Jews and the emerging community of Messiah-followers, the Imperial Cult posed a serious theological problem: participation would violate the fundamental monotheistic belief in one God and the commandment against idolatry. Recognizing this irreconcilable conflict, the Roman authorities had granted the Jewish people a special

---

[6] Mikael Tellbe, "Greco-Roman Religions and Philosophies," in *Jesus, the New Testament, and Christian Origins: Perspectives, Methods, Meanings*, ed. Dieter Mitternacht and Anders Runesson, trans. Rebecca Runesson and Noah Runesson (Grand Rapids, MI: William B. Eerdmans Publishing Company, 2021), 97.

[7] Gordon Zerbe, *Philippians*, Believers Church Bible Commentary, ed. Douglas B. Miller et al. (Harrisonburg, VA; Kitchener, ON: Herald Press, 2016), 307.

exemption (*religio licita*)⁸ from participating in the Imperial Cult. This exemption was a hard-won privilege resulting from centuries of Jewish resistance to forced assimilation under various empires. If Jewish communities paid their taxes and offered sacrifices for the emperor's well-being in the Jerusalem Temple (rather than to the emperor), they were permitted to abstain from imperial worship.⁹ This exemption created a legal and social framework within which Torah-observant Jews could navigate life in the Roman Empire while maintaining their religious integrity. However, it also created a precarious situation for the emerging Yeshua movement, particularly as it began to include increasing numbers of Gentile believers.

The Jewish Context: Identity and Boundary Markers

First-century Judaism was not a monolithic entity but a diverse religious landscape with multiple sects and traditions. The destruction of the Second Temple in 70 CE had not yet occurred, meaning that Temple worship, priesthood, and the sacrificial system were still central to Jewish religious expression. Several major groups existed within Judaism at this time:

- Pharisees: Focused on Torah interpretation and application, emphasizing ritual purity and the oral tradition alongside the written Torah.¹⁰

---

8   G. W. Clarke, "Religio Licita," in *The Anchor Yale Bible Dictionary*, ed. David Noel Freedman (New York: Doubleday, 1992), 665.
9   N. T. Wright, *Galatians*, Commentaries for Christian Formation, ed. Stephen E. Fowl, Jennie Grillo, and Robert W. Wall (Grand Rapids, MI: William B. Eerdmans Publishing Company, 2021), 24.
10 Arthur A. Cohen and Paul Mendes-Flohr, eds., *20th Century Jewish Religious Thought: Original Essays on Critical Concepts, Movements, and Beliefs* (Philadelphia, PA: The

- Sadducees: More aristocratic, conservative in their interpretation of the Torah,[11] and denied belief in resurrection and angels.
- Essenes: A separatist group focused on ritual purity and eschatological expectations, possibly connected to the Dead Sea Scrolls community.
- Zealots: Politically motivated group advocating for armed resistance against Roman occupation.[12]
- Diaspora (Hellenistic) Jews: Jews living outside the land of Israel, who balanced Torah observance with participation in Hellenistic culture.[13]

Despite their differences, these groups maintained certain common elements that defined Jewish identity. Chief among these were monotheism, Torah observance, circumcision (for males), Sabbath observance, and the dietary laws found in Leviticus 11. These practices served as "boundary markers" that distinguished Jews from their Gentile neighbors and preserved their distinct covenantal identity amidst the pressures of assimilation.[14] For Jews, these practices were not merely cultural traditions but essential expressions of covenant faithfulness to the God of Israel. Through these observances, they maintained their identity as God's chosen people, set apart from the

---

Jewish Publication Society, 2009), 1090.

11 Ibid., 1092.

12 F. L. Cross and Elizabeth A. Livingstone, eds., *The Oxford Dictionary of the Christian Church* (Oxford; New York: Oxford University Press, 2005), 1792.

13 Thomas W. Martin, "Hellenists," in *The Anchor Yale Bible Dictionary*, ed. David Noel Freedman (New York: Doubleday, 1992), 135.

14 Thomas R. Schreiner, *Paul, Apostle of God's Glory in Christ: A Pauline Theology*, 2nd ed. (Downers Grove, IL: IVP Academic: An Imprint of InterVarsity Press, 2020), 354.

nations. This understanding of covenant identity forms the backdrop for many of the controversies addressed in Galatians.

The Early Messianic Movement: A New Sect Within Judaism

The early followers of Yeshua did not initially see themselves as converting into a new religion separate from Judaism. Rather, they understood their movement as the fulfillment of Israel's eschatological hopes—the inauguration of the Messianic Age foretold by the prophets. The Greek term *ekklesia*, often translated as "church," more accurately refers to a congregation or assembly within the broader Jewish community.

The first believers were predominantly Jewish and continued to participate in Temple worship, observe Sabbath, keep kosher, and practice other Torah commandments. Acts 21:20 describes "many thousands of Jews" who were believers and were "all zealous for the Torah." The early Jerusalem community, led by James, the brother of Yeshua, maintained its Jewish character while embracing faith in Yeshua as Messiah.

The pivotal shift occurred as the message about Yeshua began to spread beyond Jewish communities to Gentiles, particularly through the ministry of Paul and others. This expansion raised unprecedented questions: How should Gentile believers relate to the Jewish roots of their faith? Were they obligated to observe Torah in the same way as Jewish believers? Did they need to undergo formal conversion (including circumcision for males) to fully participate in the covenant community?

These questions were not merely theological abstractions but had immediate practical implications. Could Jewish and Gentile believers eat together? Worship together? Intermarry? The answers would determine whether the Messianic movement would remain a Jewish sect or develop into a multi-ethnic faith community with a distinct identity.

The Crisis in Galatia: A Perfect Storm

The situation in Galatia represented a perfect storm of these theological, cultural, and political tensions. Based on the content of Paul's letter, we can reconstruct the likely sequence of events that precipitated the crisis:

1. Paul and Barnabas had established congregations in several cities of South Galatia during their first missionary journey (Acts 13–14), consisting primarily of Gentile believers with a smaller number of Jewish believers.
2. Paul had taught these believers that they were fully included in God's covenant people through faith in Messiah Yeshua, without needing to undergo formal conversion.
3. After Paul's departure, certain teachers arrived in the Galatian communities and began advocating a different position: that Gentile believers needed to undergo formal conversion, beginning with circumcision, to be fully included in God's covenant people (Gal. 3:1–3).
4. These teachers may have questioned Paul's authority, suggesting that his teaching represented a deviation from the authentic apostolic message centered in Jerusalem, and prompting him to defend his own apostolic commission as a direct revelation from God (Gal. 1:11–17).
5. Many Galatian believers were persuaded by these arguments and began to adopt Torah observance as a means of securing their place in the covenant, rather than as an expression

of their already-established covenant relationship through Messiah (Gal. 1:6–7).

Mark Johnston describes the problem that Paul was addressing in the letter thusly: "The Galatians were falling into the same trap that many have fallen into through the ages. They were trying to turn the gospel into something mechanical: reducing it to the observance of certain rituals and obedience to certain regulations. Their focus was on themselves and their own efforts rather on Christ and all he has done."[15] This new crisis in Galatia touched on multiple pressure points:

Theological Pressure

The fundamental question concerned the basis of salvation and covenant inclusion. Was faith in Messiah sufficient, or were additional works of Torah required? This theological question had profound implications for understanding God's redemptive plan and the role of the Messiah within it.[16]

Social Pressure

For Gentile believers to be fully accepted by their Jewish brothers and sisters, full conversion (including circumcision for males) would have seemed like the path of least resistance. Moreover, Jewish believers faced pressure from their non-believing Jewish community members regarding association with Gentiles who did not observe Torah, as indicated by passages such as Acts 21:29. Extending the promises of God to Abraham—as the Gospel does—was a very controversial topic

---

15   Mark Johnston, *No Longer Slaves, but Sons: A Commentary on Galatians*, Welwyn Commentary Series (Welwyn Garden City, UK: Evangelical Press, 2018), 142.
16   Ibid., 16.

in the first century, and one that carried with it the ire of many Jews, who held strict views regarding ritual conversion.[17]

Political Pressure

The Roman exemption from the Imperial Cult applied only to recognized Jews. As the Messianic movement grew more distinct from traditional Judaism while including increasingly more Gentiles, this exemption came under threat. If the movement was perceived as a new religion rather than a Jewish sect, its members could be required to participate in emperor worship or face persecution.

This complex intersection of pressures helps explain the urgency and intensity of Paul's response in Galatians. The issue was not merely theoretical but threatened the very foundation of the gospel message and the unity of the emerging Messianic community.

The Letter's Structure and Significance

Paul's letter to the Galatians follows a rhetorical structure common in the Greco-Roman world while addressing these distinctly Jewish concerns. It can be outlined as follows:

1. Introduction and expression of astonishment (1:1–10).
2. Autobiographical defense of Paul's apostolic authority (1:11–2:14).
3. Theological argument for justification by faith apart from works of law (2:15–4:31).
4. Ethical exhortation for living by the Spirit (5:1–6:10).
5. Conclusion and closing remarks (6:11–18).

---

17 Keener, *Galatians*, 27.

Throughout this structure, Paul weaves together several key themes:

The Authenticity of Paul's Gospel

Paul insists that his message came directly from divine revelation, not human instruction. This is a key point in Galatians as he contends with those that are bringing a human-centric message. This establishes his authority to address the situation in Galatia, even in opposition to others bringing their own outside influence.

The Sufficiency of Faith in Messiah

Paul emphatically argues that justification comes through faith, through the work of Messiah Yeshua, not through our human observances and works of Torah. Far from denigrating the Torah, Paul will go on to clarify that its purpose in God's redemptive plan never was to bestow eternal life to begin with.

The Unity of Jews and Gentiles in Messiah

A central concern for Paul is maintaining the unity of Jewish and Gentile believers without requiring Gentiles to become Jews or Jews to abandon their heritage. Throughout the Pauline writings, this theme of the One New Man (Eph. 2:14–16; Gal. 3:28; Col. 3:10–11) stretches across the canon to describe the unity of God's community: Jew and Gentile together, one in the Body of Messiah Yeshua. Waters' theological exposition of Ephesians sums this up succinctly and aptly, stating that, "Paul, in other words, is undertaking the work of 'identity formation,' or identity confirmation, in this letter. He wants the Ephesian Christians to have a clearer grasp of who they are in relation to Christ, the church, and the world. They need this grasp if they are to live as befits the 'one new man' that they are (2:15; cf. 4:20–21), those who have been 'created in Christ Jesus for good works, which God prepared beforehand, that we should walk in them' (2:10)."[18]

Freedom and Responsibility

Paul navigates the tension between freedom from the Torah as a means of justification and the ongoing ethical responsibility of believers to walk in love and holiness. Understanding these themes within their historical and cultural context helps us avoid common misinterpretations of Galatians. The letter is not an argument against Torah observance, but against a particular misuse of Torah as a means of justification and a prerequisite for covenant inclusion.

Relevance for Believers Today

The issues addressed in Galatians remain remarkably relevant for contemporary Messianic communities. As modern believers seek to recover the roots of their faith while maintaining the centrality of Messiah, many of the same questions resurface: How should Gentile believers relate to Torah? What practices are essential for maintaining covenant identity? How do we balance freedom in Messiah with faithfulness to God's commandments?

Galatians invites us to consider these questions thoughtfully, maintaining the proper order of precedence: first comes faith in Messiah, which establishes our covenant relationship with God, then comes obedience to Torah as an expression of that relationship, not as its basis. As we navigate these complexities, we would do well to remember Paul's ultimate concern: the preservation of the true gospel

---

[18] Guy Prentiss Waters, "Ephesians," in *A Biblical-Theological Introduction to the New Testament: The Gospel Realized*, ed. Michael J. Kruger (Wheaton, IL: Crossway, 2016), 277.

message and the unity of the body of Messiah across ethnic and cultural lines. Whatever positions we take on specific practices must serve these overarching goals.

Throughout this study of Galatians, we will see that Paul's message is not one of abandoning Torah but of properly understanding its purpose in light of Messiah's completed work. By maintaining this perspective, we can appreciate the letter's enduring significance while avoiding the interpretive errors that have often characterized its reception in Church history.

In the following chapters, we will explore Paul's arguments in detail, examining how he addresses the crisis in Galatia and articulates a vision of faith that honors both the grace of God in Messiah and the goodness of God's Torah. Our goal is not merely an intellectual exercise, wherein we gain an academic understanding, but it is also a desire to obtain a deeper appreciation of how Law and Promise work together in God's redemptive plan for humanity. As believers in Yeshua, the Scriptures are our heritage, and they are our guide—along with the Holy Spirit—in how to live our lives holy and pleasing to God.

CHAPTER 2

THE HARMONY OF THE WORD

As stated in the Introduction, our first task is to set the stage for our reexamination of the Law and the Promise. If we are to come to the text of Galatians 3 and claim—as I am—that the bulk of Christian interpretive history of this text is lacking, we must have grounds to re-open what is seemingly a closed case. Such grounds may be found in light of other texts which, when also interpreted contextually, indicate that the apostle could not be saying what the majority of his interpreters claim. Here we will turn to three passages of the New Testament.

Matthew 5 and the Perpetuity of the Torah

Matthew 5:17–20 has received much attention in recent years among Messianic and other Pronomian groups. I won't spend a lot of time on it, given the recent treatment by David Wilber in his own *Pronomian Pocket Guide* on this very passage.[1] Suffice it to say, however, that Yeshua's words that the Law was not at all abolished, and his injunction for us to not even think such a thing, should alone be cause for us to pause and reflect on an antinomian reading of Galatians 3. Even more emphatically, Messiah says that the Law and the Prophets will continue until the completion of all things. While some argue this "completion" means that the cessation of the legal obligations of the Torah occurred at the Cross,[2] it is nonsensical to view the statement in such a fashion. There is no purpose in the Messiah claiming that

---

1 David Wilber, *How Jesus Fulfilled the Law: A Pronomian Pocket Guide to Matthew 5:17–20* (Clover, SC: Pronomian Publishing, 2024).

2 Hal M. Haller Jr., "The Gospel according to Matthew," in *The Grace New Testament Commentary*, ed. Robert N. Wilkin (Denton, TX: Grace Evangelical Society, 2010), 25.

neither a large nor small thing (i.e., a "jot" or "tittle") will pass from the Law until all is fulfilled, which is paralleled with the statement that it goes on until heaven and earth pass away, if he did in fact intend for it to pass away immediately after his crucifixion.

For now, I will move on to the next passage, with just another gentle reminder that a much more robust case for Matthew 5:17–20 can be found in Wilber's book referenced above.

2 Peter and The Twisting of Paul's Words

The next logical stop along the way of building up our case for recontextualizing Galatians 3 is 2 Peter 3:14–16, which says the following:

> Therefore, beloved, since you look for these things, be diligent to be found spotless and blameless by Him, at peace, and regard the patience of our Lord as salvation; just as also our beloved brother Paul, according to the wisdom given him, wrote to you, as also in all his letters, speaking in them of these things, in which there are some things that are hard to understand, which the untaught and unstable distort, as they do also the rest of the Scriptures, to their own destruction.
> —2 Peter 3:14–16

Here I have three minor things to point out. First, the problem of interpreting Paul is not new to us believers in the twenty-first century. Even as early as the writing of 2 Peter, difficulties in interpreting his writings were already acknowledged. So, the simple fact that we ask, "Ccould we still be wrong after 2,000 years of traditional interpretation?" is not, itself, unbiblical.

Second, people were twisting the Scriptures—both Paul's letters and others—to their own destruction. To be sure, this could be read in several ways. It is possible they were twisting Scripture, as some sectarians of the first century did, to claim a special status, or to assert that salvation was achieved through certain rituals (a topic Paul spends much of Galatians arguing against). Whatever the misuse of Paul's teaching may have been, it must have been something that was destructive.

Third, the "twisters of Scripture" were untaught and unstable. Now these are tricky words to nail down. The former, ἀμαθής (*amathes*), rendered above as "untaught," is found only here in all the New Testament. In contemporary usage (such as in Philo, Josephus, Epictetus, and other Greek writers) it refers to a person who is ignorant, unlearned.[3] Here the sense is, essentially, someone who has never been taught (given the negative connection with the Greek word for disciple, one could perhaps argue that such people have never been disciples of Yeshua). The second word, ἀστήρικτος (*asteriktos*), is also a rare word, occurring only here and in 2 Peter 2:14 a chapter earlier. This word is related to the verb στηρίζω (*steridzo*), which means to strengthen or support something, such as is used in Acts 18:23 and James 5:8. The negative prefix on it means these are people who lack a stable foundation. So they are, then, those who lack a firm foundation and have not been taught or instructed in the proper meaning of Paul's writings. These are the "twisters of Scripture" in this passage.

Armed with these three points, we can keep in mind that we are in good company to question the misuse of Paul's writings and the

---

3 William Arndt, Frederick W. Danker, and Walter Bauer, *A Greek-English Lexicon of the New Testament and Other Early Christian Literature*, 3rd ed. (Chicago: University of Chicago Press, 2000), 49.

other Scriptures by those who are lacking a firm foundation and are untaught.

Acts 21: A Case Study in Torah Observance

If there were a single passage I would point to as an example of the believer's ongoing obligation to keep the Law even after Christ's resurrection, it would be Acts 21. Here again, much like with Matthew 5:17–20, I will not expend much ink. A much fuller and better treatment of Acts 21:20–36 can be found in G. Scott McKenzie's *Pronomian Pocket Guide* on this passage.[4]

For my purposes here and now, I would bid the reader take a moment to pause and read the verses in question. The narrative plainly makes my case, I believe, but I will summarize it here. Paul goes back to Jerusalem and the other apostles meet him and tell him that the people of the city have been hearing rumors that he teaches against the Law. To prove that this rumor is not true, the Jerusalem apostles instruct Paul to go and offer the sacrifice offered at the completion of a vow alongside a few men who had just completed their own vows, and to be cleansed with them. This participation in the Temple offering would surely demonstrate to the people in Jerusalem that Paul did not, in fact, believe in abandoning the Law.

Would it be possible for Paul, who goes so far as to engage in the Temple's sacrificial system to disprove these antinomian rumors, to then also simultaneously be teaching the very same things of which he has been denying herein? The same Paul who was willing to even stand up against Peter in opposition to Peter's own hypocrisy (Gal.

---

[4] G. Scott McKenzie, *Walking Orderly, Keeping the Law: A Pronomian Pocket Guide to Acts 21:20–26* (Clover, SC: Pronomian Publishing, 2024).

2:11–14)? I posit that such a reading is not only untenable in terms of the consistency and integrity of Scripture, but it also serves only to produce a Paul who is of two minds, a sort of theological schizophrenia.

Reframing "Under the Law"

Having laid the foundation on but a handful of additional Scriptures, we need to also frame our understanding of the key phrase that will be examined within this book: "under the law." Far too many commentators have taken it simply to mean "obedient to the Law of Moses." This popular interpretation is common, but greatly problematic. Not only is it lacking in contextual depth, it also even leads to more philosophical and exegetical gymnastics being needed to explain *how much* of the law need not be obeyed. In Thomas Aquinas' massive work *Summa Theologica*, he sets about defining the difference in the division of the Old Testament Law into three categories. These would, over time, be further developed into the major categories we see so often still used today: civil, ceremonial, and moral. The convenient explanation used by many churchgoers over the centuries has been that the moral laws of the Torah are eternal and immutable, so things like rape, murder, and theft will always be immoral. Meanwhile, ceremonial laws were only shadows and representations of later realities, like ritual cleansing, food laws, and sacrifices. These—so we are told— were done away in Christ's death and resurrection. Lastly, there are civil laws that pertained to the Land of Israel under the former Jewish monarchy, and were time-bound, meaning abrogated when Rome destroyed the Temple and exiled the people in 70 C.E.

As nice and neat as this may well sound—and indeed, it is at least well thought out on the surface—it is nonetheless lacking in depth. For instance, does the Torah's injunction against wearing a garment of linen mixed with wool (Lev. 19:19; Deut. 22:11) fall into the civil, ceremonial, or moral bucket? Many would say ceremonial, but there is no direct ceremonial practice tied to it, nor is it for priests and Levites alone, nor does it relate to the Temple or Tabernacle. Further, if the statute that prohibits mistreating orphans, widows, and foreigners is a moral imperative—as is stated in Exodus 22:22—is it not a strictly civil law in Deuteronomy 24:19–20, where it is explicitly tied to harvests within the land of Israel, and leaving the gleanings for those on the outskirts of society? Additionally, if some laws are moral, does that somehow imply others are not? Would God issue a commandment, statute, or ordinance that is not moral? The author of Psalm 119 went to great poetic and scribal lengths to assert vehemently the opposite: namely, that all God's laws and commandments and statutes and ordinances are righteous (vs. 75), faithful (vs. 86), true (vs. 142), and the author's delight and love. All of God's commandments reflect his character and his nature, and as such they are all good.

So how, then, can Paul—the very apostle of the Gentiles himself—come along and say that believers are not "under the law"? Romans 6:14–15 is often taken alongside Galatians 3 to make this very point, that believers today are not obligated to obey the Torah. But is that what Paul means? Could it even be consistent with what we have read in this chapter so far? I suggest that it is not. As such, we must try to ascertain an interpretation and understanding of the phrase "under the law" that sits in harmony with Paul's teachings elsewhere and with the whole of Scripture.

With that in mind then, I propose that "under the law" does not refer simply to some sort of obligation to keep the Torah. Rather, I assert that "under the law" (υπο νομον in Greek) is a reference to a particular orientation and sphere of jurisdiction of the Torah.

CHAPTER 3

UNDER WHAT, EXACTLY?

As stated in the previous chapter, "under the law" in Galatians—and Romans 6 for that matter—should not be taken to be synonymous with keeping or observing the Torah. This might come as a surprise to many readers, given how frequently this phrase has been used throughout Christian history to suggest that Torah observance is no longer required for believers in Messiah. One much more critical scholar even goes so far as to claim that Paul never taught that God gave the Torah, but rather that it was given by a demonic host (which, he argues, Paul identifies as the angels who mediated the giving of the Torah in Gal. 3:19), and that this is why the apostle is so quick and apt to dispense with it.[1] I believe most of the readers of the present volume, however, would not go so far as to make such a claim. Yet, nevertheless, the negative sense in which the Torah is viewed by so many scholars—even evangelical scholars—is not lost here. For instance, Michael Burer similarly sides with the negative view in his 2024 Evangelical Exegetical Commentary, claiming that the giving of the Torah had the purpose of provoking transgression.[2] Thus, Israel was placed "under the law" in order to bring about an acute awareness of sin, but with the consequence that such an awareness would cause sin.

However, a careful examination of Scripture reveals that in all its uses in the Greek New Testament, the phrase "under the law" (*hypo nomon*) never actually refers to a believer's obligation to obey God's command-

---

1   Hans Hübner, *Law in Paul's Thought* (London; New York: T&T Clark, 1984), 24-36.
2   Michael H. Burer, *Galatians*, Evangelical Exegetical Commentary, ed. Tremper Longman III, Andreas J. Köstenberger, and Benjamin L. Gladd (Bellingham, WA: Lexham Academic, 2024), 303.

ments. Further, the phrase is never used by God nor used by any Biblical writer to describe a state wherein God causes his people to transgress his commandments.

Examining "Under the Law" in the New Testament

Among all the passages of the New Testament, the phrase "under the law" appears in only eight places (Rom. 6:14–15, 1 Cor. 9:20, and the other five in Galatians). What is particularly striking is that in each of these instances, it is used in a negative sense. That is, it conveys something undesirable: believers should *not* want to be "under the law."

In Romans 6, Paul states that believers are *not* under law, as they are under grace. The implication here is that being "under grace" is the antithesis of being "under the law." In Galatians, Paul makes repeated corrective comments, such as in Galatians 4:21, where he speaks to those who "want to be under the law." Once again, being "under the law" is portrayed as problematic. In 1 Corinthians 9:20, Paul says that he is not under the law, but he became *like* one under the law in order to win over those who are under the law. Paul denies being, in reality, under the law because being so is, once again, presented as a negative condition.

Biblical scholar Brian Rosner notes this well, stating that "in Galatians, however, and in Romans Paul uses 'under the law' more negatively and his response to such a condition is far from neutral. Even if the Galatian believers sought to live 'under the law'...Paul warns them that such a move entails something far more worrying if it is seen as additional to faith in and union with Christ."[3]

---

3   Brian S. Rosner, *Paul and the Law: Keeping the Commandments of God*, vol. 31, New Studies in Biblical Theology, ed. D. A. Carson (Downers Grove, IL; England: InterVarsity Press; Apollos, 2013), 57.

Rosner aptly identifies that, in both Romans and especially Galatians, Paul emphasizes that believers should not be "under the law." This should give us pause—if Paul is adamant that we should not be "under the law," yet elsewhere affirms the goodness and holiness of the Torah (Rom. 7:12), we must be missing something in our understanding of this phrase.[4]

What "Under the Law" Really Means

So what, then, does "under the law" mean? This requires us to dig a bit deeper into the text and context of Paul's writings.

Being "under the law" encompasses several interconnected concepts. First, it means being subject to the legal jurisdiction of the Torah—that is, being liable for breaking it. As Paul explains in Romans 1, even those without the Torah itself are without excuse when it comes to committing sin, since the Torah has jurisdiction over humanity in a legal sense (as Paul also affirms in Romans 7). To be "under the law" is to be subject to its penalties and judgments.

However, there is more to Torah than just legal codes and punishments; there is also a covenantal framework to it. The very beginning of the giving of the Torah from Sinai, starting with the Ten Commandments, records God saying "I am the LORD your God, who brought you out of the land of Egypt..." (Exod. 20:2). This is covenant language that establishes relationship before requirements. It is repeated throughout the Torah. Even when Israel rebels and breaks the Torah and turns to other gods, the Lord still reminds them of the covenant relationship throughout the Prophets (Isaiah, Jeremiah, Hosea, and others). God

---

[4] As an aside, Rosner's ultimate conclusion varies quite a bit from mine, as he maintains continuity with the predominant interpretation that considers Torah-keeping is not obligatory for believers today

establishes his relationship with his people *prior* to telling them what "rules" to follow.

This pattern is evident in the Abrahamic covenant as well. In Genesis 15, we find God calling to Abram and promising him blessings and an heir (Gen. 15:1–4) even before giving covenantal laws to him. Scripture tells us that "Abram believed the Lord, and it was reckoned to him as righteousness" (Gen. 15:6). The sign of circumcision is not instituted until after this, after the covenant of the pieces. The work, *or law*, of circumcision, and the requirement for the males in Abraham's household to be circumcised, came *after* the relationship with God was established.

So, too, do we find in Paul's teaching: the promise came first (Gal. 3:15–16) and then the Torah was given after that (Gal. 3:17–22). The entire premise of the promise of being God's people is built not on the Mosaic covenant, but on the Abrahamic covenant. The promised seed (Isaac in one sense, but ultimately, as Paul says in Galatians 3:16, Yeshua) was to come as the culmination of the covenant with Abraham, bringing blessing to all nations. Rabbi Eric Tokajer, commenting on Galatians 3:19, writes the following:

> Now, it is important to note that these laws did not ever provide salvation, nor were they ever meant to provide a way of salvation or a key to beginning a relationship with God. The Torah is the result of a relationship with God. Another way to say this would be that Israel didn't keep the Torah to have a covenant relationship with God, rather God gave them the Torah because they were already in a covenant relationship with Him. Likewise, as believers in Messiah Yeshua today, we don't keep the Torah to achieve or earn salvation or redemp-

tion, but rather we keep the Torah because we have been redeemed.[5]

Under the Law: Legal Obligations and Jurisdiction

To summarize, then, being under the law means being within its sphere of authority, in its jurisdiction. This has a protective and covenantal sense, but also a legal (and by extension, judgmental) sense. Within the realm of relationship with God, the Torah carries legal expectations and judgments. Being "under the law" includes being subject to the legal punishments and judgments that the law imposes on the lawbreaker.

This understanding helps us make sense of another puzzling passage. Yeshua himself was also born "under the law" as Paul says in Galatians 4:

> Now I say, as long as the heir is a child, he does not differ at all from a slave, although he is owner of everything, but he is under guardians and managers until the date set by the father. So we too, when we were children, were held in bondage under the elementary principles of the world. But when the fullness of the time came, God sent His Son, born of a woman, born under the Law, so that He might redeem those who were under the Law, that we might receive the adoption as sons and daughters.
> —Galatians 4:1–5

We will examine the "guardians and managers" in chapter 4. For now, I want to focus on how Yeshua was born "under the law" to

---

5   Eric D. Tokajer, *Galatians in Context* (Pensacola, FL: Eric Tokajer, 2019), 91.

redeem those under the law. This raises an important question: Did Yeshua's work only redeem Jewish people? Certainly not, as Scripture clearly proclaims that Yeshua's work of redemption is for all, whether Jewish or not. So, if he redeemed those under the law, then "under the law" cannot simply refer exclusively to Jews.[6]

Under the Law: Under Its Curse

The difficulty in resolving this issue begins to dissipate when we carefully examine the terminology of being "under the law." First, the phrase "under the law" refers to being subject to its curse. Carefully note that this does not imply that the Torah itself is a curse, but rather that disobedience to the Torah results in death, a concept on which Paul elaborates extensively in Galatians 3 and Romans 6–8. As Todd Wilson observes, Paul writes within a framework where "under the law" likely serves as a shorthand reference for "under the curse of the law," signifying the penalty one incurs for breaking the Torah.[7] Thus, understood in this way, being not "under the law" does not refer to a believer's "get out of Torah free" card; rather, it refers to us—in Yeshua—being not bound by the curse that the Torah brings to those who break it. This understanding raises a second consideration regarding Messiah being born "under the law." At first glance, this presents a theological conundrum: if "under the law" refers exclusively to those bound by the curse and penalty of law-breaking, then how could Yeshua have been born "under the law" when he was without sin (1 Pet. 2:22; Heb. 4:15)? The answer, I submit, is found in 2 Corinthians 5:21, which states, "He

---

[6] This is addressed more fully in Appendix A, where 1 Corinthians 9 is discussed and how the phrase "under the law" there refers to more than just Jews.

[7] Todd Wilson, "Under Law in Galatians: A Pauline Theological Abbreviation," *Journal of Theological Studies* 56 (2005), 363.

made Him who knew no sin *to be* sin in our behalf, so that we might become the righteousness of God in Him" (2 Cor. 5:21).

Yeshua took on *our* sin, and in doing so, he incurred the curse of the Law for our sake. As Paul declares, "Messiah redeemed us from the curse of the Law, having become a curse for us...in order that in Messiah Yeshua the blessing of Abraham would come to the Gentiles, so that we would receive the promise of the Spirit through faith" (Gal. 3:13–14). By being "born under the [curse of] the law," Yeshua subjected himself to the penalties of the Torah when he took on the curse for us.

A Lingering Question Resolved

A lingering question may persist even after accepting the explanation provided above: if being "under the law" is inherently negative, signifying subjection to the penalties of law-breaking, why would anyone advocate returning to such a state? That is, after all, what Paul's letter to the Galatians addresses: some members of the Galatian congregation were being persuaded to return to *something* that included living "under the law." Paul was passionately warning them against this course of action, insisting they *do not* want to be "under the law."

If being "under the law" is a negative condition, why would anyone promote it? The answer lies in recognizing the specific error Paul was addressing. The individuals in question were attempting to assign the Torah a role it was never intended to have: mediating righteousness between God and humanity. They sought to use the Torah as a means of achieving salvation, effectively advocating for a form of "entrance into the Kingdom through law-keeping" that bypassed the necessity of faith in, and the faithfulness of, the Messiah.

By pursuing righteousness through ritual observance and formal conversion, they were abandoning the core tenets of the faith. The central issue throughout Galatians is precisely this: attempting to use the Torah to gain right standing with God (i.e., justification), instead of obtaining right standing through Yeshua. The concern then is not that the people in question wanted to be cursed, or even to be "under the law" in the strict sense. However, that would be the ultimate consequence if they continued down the path they were on by abandoning trust in Yeshua as the sole means of salvation.

Torah Observance vs. Being "Under the Law"

Having observed that being "under the law" does not refer to keeping the Torah, we can now state more clearly what this means for believers today. A believer has an obligation to obey God in accordance with the revelation they have received. As such, this includes observing the precepts of the Torah when and where and how one is able to do so.[8] While commonly used as an argument against Torah-keeping for believers today, the phrase "under the law" does not, in fact, refer to keeping the Torah, but rather to trying to use the Torah for gaining right-standing with God outside of Messiah.

This distinction is crucial for several reasons. First, it maintains the integrity of Paul's theological framework, where the Torah is "holy, righteous, and good" (Rom. 7:12) even while he warns against seeking justification through it. Second, it aligns with passages like Acts 21, where Paul himself participates in Temple rituals to demonstrate his continued commitment to Torah observance. Third, it harmonizes with Yeshua's teaching that not even the smallest stroke of the Law would pass away

---

8   While outside the scope of the present work, it should be noted that there is no human in history to which all the Torah's requirements have ever applied. Some apply only to priests, others only to monarchs, others only to women, and so forth. Simply put, if there are 613 commandments in the Torah, only a portion of them are applicable to the life of the believer. So while they are morally obligatory, they are also contextual and must be understood and observed in a proper, Messiah-shaped way.

until heaven and earth pass away (Matt. 5:18). Moreover, this understanding challenges the common notion that Paul was advocating for an abandonment of Torah observance. Rather, he was warning against a fundamental misuse of the Torah—attempting to use it as a means of justification rather than receiving justification through faith in Messiah. The Torah was never designed to be a means of salvation; it was given to a people already in covenant relationship with God, as a guide for living within that relationship.

With this in mind, all believers can and should firmly agree with the apostle Paul here: we do not want to be "under the law." We do not want to be subject to the curse and penalty that the Torah prescribes for those who break it. Instead, we want to be under grace, receiving the righteousness that comes through faith in Messiah Yeshua. At the same time, as those who have been set free from the curse of the law, we are empowered by the Spirit to fulfill the righteous requirements of the Torah (Rom. 8:4), not as a means of justification, but as an expression of our love for God and our desire to walk in his ways.

This nuanced understanding of "under the law" allows us to affirm both the continuing validity of the Torah for believers today and the central New Testament teaching that justification comes through faith in Messiah alone. It enables us to appreciate Paul's warnings in Galatians without concluding that he was opposed to Torah observance itself. As we will explore in subsequent chapters, the Torah continues to play vital roles in the lives of believers, even as it is no longer the source of our righteousness before God.

CHAPTER 4

GUARDIANS AND MANAGERS

> But before faith came, we were kept in custody under the Law, being confined for the faith that was destined to be revealed. Therefore the Law has become our guardian to lead us to Christ, so that we may be justified by faith. But now that faith has come, we are no longer under a guardian.
>
> Now I say, as long as the heir is a child, he does not differ at all from a slave, although he is owner of everything, but he is under guardians and managers until the date set by the father. So we too, when we were children, were held in bondage under the elementary principles of the world. But when the fullness of the time came, God sent His Son, born of a woman, born under the Law, so that He might redeem those who were under the Law, that we might receive the adoption as sons and daughters. Because you are sons, God has sent the Spirit of His Son into our hearts, crying out, "Abba! Father!" Therefore you are no longer a slave, but a son; and if a son, then an heir through God.
> —Galatians 3:23–4:7

Without Yeshua all humanity is left without hope, without a means of salvation. Even having the Torah, Israel did not have salvation outside of trusting in the eternal God. Paul reiterates much the same here in Galatians 4 and further clarifies that the Torah serves a guardianship role to lead us to Messiah, but it is not the life-giver itself. In this chapter, we will explore the rich metaphors Paul employs to describe the Torah's function, particularly focusing on the terms "guardian," "manager," and "steward." Understanding these metaphors is crucial for grasping Paul's view of the Torah's role in God's redemptive plan. Many scholars argue that Galatians 4 is where Paul doubles down on his argument against Torah observance. Soards and Pursiful state this overtly, saying "In chapter 4 Paul continues to argue against the necessity—or even the desirability—of Law observance for his Galatian Gentile converts to Christianity."[1] Yet as we have noted, and will continue to highlight, this is not the case.

Apart from Yeshua, the issue and problem of sin is not dealt with, and as such we remain confined in custody and imprisoned (Gal. 3:23), owing the penalty of sin (i.e., the curse of the law). This of course makes sense; the Torah's purpose here is to confine and imprison, not to set free, as freedom from sin comes as a divine action. Yeshua alone frees from sin, so while our own sins—our own Torah-breaking—is what lands us in spiritual jail, it is the work of Yeshua that puts an end to the sentence against us. McKee summarizes this note (and Gal. 3:23 as a whole) thusly: "A proper view of Galatians 3:23 recognizes that: (1) saving faith is to manifest itself in the life of a Believer, (2) because of such faith one is freed from the imprisoning condemnation of sin and being 'under law,' and (3) this results in being revealed a greater significance of faith as growth in Messiah begins."[2]

Notice well, too, what Paul does *not* assert however: he does not claim the Torah ceases to have function with the coming of Messiah. He states that one of the Torah's roles is to serve as a guardian or

---

[1] Marion L. Soards and Darrell J. Pursiful, *Galatians*, Smyth & Helwys Bible Commentary, ed. R. Alan Culpepper (Macon, GA: Smyth & Helwys Publishing, Inc., 2015), 187.

[2] J. K. McKee, Galatians for the Practical Messianic (McKinney, TX: Outreach Israel, 2012), 164.

manager. This is not the Torah's only role, but it is one of its functions, and this role is temporal in a very logical sense. If the Torah's goal is to lead us to Messiah, then by the very definition of that purpose, that very role ceases when we come to Messiah, as we have already arrived at the goal. And while one of the purposes of the Torah is, indeed, to lead us to Messiah, it is not the only purpose, though these will be explored further in Chapter 5.

The Torah as Guardian: Analyzing Paul's Metaphor

One of the most significant and often misunderstood metaphors in Galatians is Paul's description of the Torah as a "guardian" or "tutor." This metaphor has frequently been interpreted to mean that the Torah was a harsh, restrictive force from which believers have now been liberated. However, a closer examination of the terms Paul uses reveals a more nuanced and positive understanding of the Torah's role.

In Galatians 3:23–25, Paul uses the Greek word παιδαγωγός (*paidagogos*), commonly translated as "tutor" or "guardian." This term refers to a specific role in Greco-Roman society, typically performed by a slave who was entrusted with the care and supervision of a child from approximately age six to sixteen. (This word is also borrowed over into later Rabbinic works.)[3] The *paidagogos* was responsible for accompanying the child to school, supervising their behavior, and instructing them in proper social conduct and manners. Importantly, while the *paidagogos* had disciplinary authority, their role was fundamentally protective and educational, designed to guide the child toward maturity and prepare them for adult responsibilities. This cultural background illuminates Paul's use of the metaphor. The Torah, like the *paidagogos*,

---

3 Horst Robert Balz and Gerhard Schneider, *Exegetical Dictionary of the New Testament* (Grand Rapids, Mich.: Eerdmans, 1990), 2.

was not a harsh taskmaster but a divinely appointed guide, entrusted with the care and instruction of God's people until they reached "maturity" in Messiah. The *paidagogos* metaphor underscores both the temporary nature of this particular function of the Torah (it applies specifically to the period before faith in Messiah) and its positive, preparatory purpose.

In discussing this passage in Galatians 3, Thomas Schreiner notes, "Furthermore, the Mosaic law is a temporary covenant, and it is subsidiary to the covenant with Abraham (3:15–25); hence, believers are no longer under its authority. They are now God's sons and heirs, not by observing the law but through faith in Christ and by virtue of union with Christ (3:26–4:7)."[4] While Schreiner rightly emphasizes the Abrahamic covenant as that which covers the promise, and adoption as sons and daughters of God through Messiah, he—along with most others holding the traditional view—misses the mark by not recognizing the distinction between the temporary function of the Torah, versus the Torah itself. Despite this disagreement about the mechanism and the functions (yes, plural) of the Torah, we can at least agree with Schreiner on his later point: "Therefore, at the end of the day, the law and the gospel work together, and both fit harmoniously into the one plan of God."[5]

Expanding the Metaphor: Guardians and Managers

In Galatians 4:2, Paul introduces two additional terms to further elaborate on the Torah's role within the divine economy: ἐπίτροπος (*epitropos*), commonly translated as "guardian," and οἰκονόμος

---

[4] Thomas R. Schreiner, *Galatians*, Zondervan Exegetical Commentary on the New Testament (Grand Rapids, MI: Zondervan, 2010), 281.

[5] Ibid., 396

(*oikonomos*), rendered as "steward" or "manager." These terms enrich our understanding of the Torah's function beyond what is conveyed by *paidagogos* alone.

The term ἐπίτροπος (*epitropos*) is more general than *paidagogos* and refers to someone entrusted with oversight or guardianship in various contexts. In Greco-Roman society, an *epitropos* could be a guardian appointed for orphaned children, a steward managing an estate, or even a provincial governor.[6] The common thread is the exercise of delegated authority on behalf of someone else. In the context of Galatians 4, the *epitropos* represents the Torah's function in providing legal oversight and protection for God's people during their spiritual "childhood."

The second term, οἰκονόμος (*oikonomos*), refers specifically to a household manager or steward—someone responsible for administering the practical affairs of a household or estate. The *oikonomos* would oversee servants, manage finances, and ensure the efficient operation of the household. This metaphor highlights the Torah's role in ordering and structuring the daily life of the covenant community, providing a framework for worship, ethics, and social relationships.[7]

Together, these three terms—*paidagogos, epitropos,* and *oikonomos*—paint a comprehensive picture of the Torah's multifaceted role in God's redemptive plan. The Torah guided, protected, and structured the life of Israel, preparing them for the coming of Messiah. Far from being solely a harsh or negative force, the Torah functioned as a divinely appointed guardian, entrusted with the care and preparation of God's people.

---

6   Henry George Liddell, et al., *A Greek-English Lexicon* (Oxford: Clarendon Press, 1996), 669.
7   Ibid., 1204.

The Household Analogy: Understanding the Torah's Role

To better grasp Paul's complex metaphor, consider the analogy of an ancient household with its various supervisory roles. Each role Paul references had distinct yet overlapping functions in the upbringing and protection of children in the household.

The *paidagogos* (tutor or custodian) corresponds to the Torah's role in guiding, instructing, and disciplining Israel, shaping their moral, social, and communal life in accordance with God's standards. This role was deeply formative, ensuring that the people of God were trained in righteousness and prepared for their eventual inheritance. The *epitropos* (guardian) reflects the Torah's broader oversight, serving as a legal and covenantal framework that ensures Israel's adherence to their obligations under the covenant. This role is more administrative, providing structure and accountability for the congregation. Finally, the *oikonomos* (manager or steward) symbolizes the Torah's function in ordering the practical, day-to-day life of the assembly, ensuring that the household of God operates in a manner that reflects his character.

Together, these roles represent subordinate but essential functions within the household, each contributing to the upbringing and preparation of the heir—the people of God—until the time of maturity. The key point of this analogy is that these roles, while vital, are inherently temporary and preparatory in a specific sense. Just as a child, during the time of childhood, is subject to tutors, guardians, and stewards who guide and govern their conduct, so too was Israel under the custodial authority of the Torah. However, upon reaching maturity, the child no longer relates to these figures in the same way; they step into their full inheritance and assume the responsibilities of adulthood.

It is crucial to understand that the transition from childhood to adulthood in this analogy does not mean the child no longer respects or learns from their former guardians, nor do they completely reject him. Rather, the relationship is transformed—what was once a relationship of subordination becomes one of mature appreciation. In the same way, the coming of Messiah transforms our relationship to the Torah without negating its value or ongoing relevance. We gain a new relationship to the Torah as the Law of Messiah, and we walk the Torah out in a Messiah-shaped way.

The Temporal Nature of the Guardian Function

A key aspect of Paul's metaphor is its temporal dimension. Just as the *paidagogos*, *epitropos*, and *oikonomos* had authority over a child only until the "time set by the father" (Gal. 4:2), so too the Torah's role as guardian was designed to last until the coming of faith in Messiah. When Paul states that "now that faith has come, we are no longer under a guardian" (Gal. 3:25), he is not declaring the Torah obsolete but rather indicating a transformation in how believers relate to it.

The temporary nature of the guardian function should not be confused with the abrogation of the Torah itself. Rather, it refers specifically to one particular function of the Torah—its role in leading people to recognize their need for Messiah. This function is, by its very definition, fulfilled when a person comes to faith in Messiah. The person has arrived at the destination to which the Torah was guiding them. This maturation doesn't mean abandoning the wisdom and guidance of the Torah, but rather embracing it in a new way, empowered by the Spirit and guided by Messiah's example.

In addition to the aspects mentioned in the present chapter, as previously stated, we will sum up the additional facets of the purpose(s) for the Torah in chapter 5.

CHAPTER 5

BACK TO BASICS

To adequately situate ourselves within the framework of Paul's writings, we must be willing to engage with the intellectual paradigms that shaped the apostle's own thought and methodology. Paul, as a first-century Jewish scholar and rhetorician, possessed theological and exegetical skills that would rival the top PhDs of today's world (to say nothing of his own special revelation and apostolic ordination). His extensive training under Gamaliel, a prominent Pharisaic teacher (Acts 22:3), and his profound expertise in the Hebrew Scriptures set him up to be a formidable theological mind within his Jewish context. As a result, to grasp the nuances of Paul's teachings, we must first establish a framework of understanding that accounts for the textual and theological traditions that informed his worldview. By properly understanding this framework we begin to get a clearer glimpse into Paul's writings and can appreciate the depth of his engagement with the Hebrew Scriptures. We want to engage with how Paul teaches Law, promise, and covenant in Galatians.

Abraham's Faith and God's Promise

One of the key passages in Galatians is about Abraham's faith, and how God reckoned it to him as righteousness. This is a very important passage for Paul (and for James—see James 2:23—though that is beyond the scope of our present endeavor). For Paul, the promise of life in Yeshua cannot be boiled down to rote, mechanical religion. As such, Torah observance and reliance on one's own works is not sufficient for salvation: only Yeshua saves. Period. This is important to note, especially for Torah observant believers who tend to focus so much of our time and attention on matters of law and keeping the Torah. Paul does not find the promise of life everlasting in Mount Sinai. Rather, he locates it in faith; Abraham's faith, and the promise that was made to Abraham. When Paul refers to covenant and promise in Galatians, he refers to the covenant with Abraham, as he is writing to a predominantly Gentile audience. This Gentile audience was being invited to participate in God's covenant with Abraham through Yeshua, just as God promised Abraham that he would bless all nations through his Seed (which, again, Paul identifies as Yeshua).

The Sarah-Hagar Allegory: Misinterpretations and Clarifications

A crucial element for understanding the nuances of Paul's theology of Law and Promise here lies in the story of Ishmael and Hagar, particularly as Paul employs this story in Galatians 4. This allegory has frequently been misappropriated throughout Church history to elevate Sarah as an archetype of Christian virtue while relegating Hagar to a symbol for Jewish rejection of Messiah. Antisemitic undertones and their implications aside—as well as the glaringly obvious irony in referring to Sarah who was, herself, a Matriarch of the Jewish people—this allegory has remained profoundly perplexing, especially to those in the Messianic walk and those adjacent to it. The way the narrative is construed by Paul does seem to indicate that he pits Sarah (Promise) over and against Hagar (Law). But that is not what is being presented here. To properly comprehend the Law-Promise relationship and how it features in Paul's Sarah-Hagar allegory, we first need to revisit and reexamine the source material from which Paul draws his teaching: the Genesis narrative.

The Genesis Narrative: Context and Significance

Genesis 15 records God's covenant promise to Abram regarding a son who would be his direct heir. In Genesis 16, we encounter Sarai—

believing herself to be permanently barren due to divine intervention ("The Lord has prevented me from bearing children," Gen. 16:2)—imploring Abram to conceive a child with Hagar, her Egyptian slave. This son would then serve as a surrogate heir for Abram and Sarai, fulfilling the divine promise through human means. Abram acquiesces to Sarai's proposition seemingly without protest (or if there was, we are not told of it), and the narrative unfolds with profound emotional, spiritual, and relational consequences, affecting not only Abram and Sarai but arguably afflicting greater suffering on Hagar and Ishmael.

Ishmael's conception and birth emerged not because of faithful obedience and trust in God's promise, but rather from human intervention. This was essentially a premature attempt to bring about God's covenant promise through unauthorized and humanly means. Though Abram and Sarai genuinely desired the promised heir, they substituted faith in God for human machination. They tried to force the promise to come about by having Abram raise up a son with Hagar. The narrative eventually culminates with Sarah (after the theologically significant renaming of both her and Abraham) conceiving and bearing the legitimate covenant heir, Isaac, "the son of promise." This narrative trajectory forms the essential foundation and conceptual framework of Paul's allegorical application in Galatians.

Notably, the original narrative in Genesis does not cast Sarah as a moral exemplar and Hagar as a villainess or usurper. Not at all, in fact God himself goes to meet with Hagar and tends to her, and promises her and her son blessings as well, even after Sarah abuses her. The divine promise to Hagar that "I will so greatly multiply your offspring that they cannot be counted for multitude" (Gen. 16:10) parallels the promises made to Abram himself, indicating that Hagar and Ishmael—while outside the primary covenant lineage—remain beneficiaries of divine blessing and provision. Now, like any good metaphor (or allegory), there is only so much that is intended by the author. For the modern reader then, we must carefully discern the point Paul is making in using Sarah and Hagar in this way, as well as understand the limitations to this reference, avoiding overly simplistic or reductive readings. So, with that, let us take to task the relevant passages of Galatians 4 once again.

Paul's Allegorical Interpretation

First, Paul addresses those who "want to be under the law" (Gal. 4:21). As previously stated, in this he is addressing people who desire to live by mechanical means, not by faith like Abraham (you could say, those who believe religious actions will save them, rather than their loyal profession of allegiance to King Yeshua). Second, he contrasts the women's legal statuses: one free (Sarah) and the other a slave (Hagar). The slave woman bore a son according to the flesh, while the free woman bore a son through the promise (vs. 23). What follows is Paul's contrast of the birth "according to the flesh" vs. the birth "according to the promise." That which is according to the flesh he connects to Mount Sinai and the "present Jerusalem." That according to the promise, he says, is the Jerusalem "from above; she is our mother." Once again, the emphasis here is not Torah vs. promise as if the two are at odds; it is about the utilization of Torah and human action (works) as a means of trying to force God to fulfill an obligation, vs. the faithfulness of Messiah in completing the work he came to do.

The Heart of Paul's Argument

The central point Paul makes, overall, is this: just as Abraham failed to attain the promise by trying to work and do it himself (via Hagar), so too does justification not come by our own works of mechanical religion. No amount of kosher-eating or Sabbath-keeping will obligate God to grant one salvation, as salvation comes only through Yeshua. The reference to the "present Jerusalem" vs. the "Jerusalem from above" is similar: a contrast of a lesser to a greater reality, and a reference that Paul makes to highlight the eschatological superiority of the Jerusalem from above.[1] The entry on "The Jerusalem Above" from the *Dictionary of Paul and His Letters* is particularly noteworthy here:

> This spiritual, eschatological Jerusalem is bound up therefore with the risen Lord Jesus and his Spirit's presence in the hearts of Christ's people (Gal 4:4–6). A place in this Jerusalem implies adoption and inheritance as God's sons (Gal 4:7), the rejoicing foreseen by Isaiah as promises for Zion are fulfilled (Gal 4:27–28), and "the hope of righteousness" (Gal 5:5). In this way, the new Jerusalem is for Paul an integral image reflecting believers' new status as heirs with Christ and anticipating life in the new creation (see also Heb 12:22–24; Rev 3:12, 21).[2]

Application to the Galatian Context

Paul's use of the Sarah-Hagar allegory directly addressed the situation in the Galatian congregation, where some believers were being persuaded to seek justification through Torah observance rather than

---

1 For more on this, see Hebrews 11:10, 12:22, and Philipians 3:20, as these also refer to a heavenly Jerusalem in which believers have citizenship. This is an example of a "Now, but not yet" sort of eschatology that is frequently found in Paul's writings, where he speaks both of a present reality as well as that which is to come at the culmination of time, with the Kingdom of Yeshua.

2 David K. Burge, "Jerusalem, City Of," in *Dictionary of Paul and His Letters: A Compendium of Contemporary Biblical Scholarship*, ed. Scot McKnight (Downers Grove, IL: IVP Academic: An Imprint of InterVarsity Press, 2023), 546.

through faith in Messiah. By returning to the foundational Abrahamic narrative, Paul reminds his readers that the pattern of justification by faith was established long before even the giving of the Torah at Sinai.

The Galatian believers, mostly Gentiles, needed to understand that their inclusion in God's covenant people came not through adopting Jewish identity such as circumcision (i.e., ritual conversion did not grant them salvation), but through faith in Messiah Yeshua. Like Isaac, they were "children of promise" (Gal. 4:28), born not of natural descent or human effort but through the miraculous work of God's Spirit.

This did not mean, however, that the Torah was irrelevant to their lives as believers. Rather, it meant that they related to the Torah not as a means of justification but as a guide for living as God's covenant people. The Torah continued to reveal God's character and will, but its commands were to be fulfilled through the power of the Spirit rather than through human effort alone. The promise of a future New Covenant, prophesied through Jeremiah and Ezekiel, anticipated an ongoing observance of the Torah, but through a new orientation of a circumcised heart:

> "Behold, days are coming," declares the Lord, "when I will make a new covenant with the house of Israel and the house of Judah, not like the covenant which I made with their fathers on the day I took them by the hand to bring them out of the land of Egypt, My covenant which they broke, although I was a husband to them," declares the Lord. "For this is the covenant which I will make with the house of Israel after those days," declares the Lord: "I will put My law within them and write it on their heart; and I will be their God, and they shall be My people. They will not teach again, each one

his neighbor and each one his brother, saying, 'Know the Lord,' for they will all know Me, from the least of them to the greatest of them," declares the Lord, "for I will forgive their wrongdoing, and their sin I will no longer remember."
—Jeremiah 31:31–34

The prophets speak of a time when the Torah is written on the heart, and when all people will know the Lord.

Contemporary Relevance: Avoiding False Dichotomies

For contemporary believers, Paul's teaching on the Sarah-Hagar allegory offers several important insights:

1. The danger of self-justification: Like Abraham and Sarah's attempt to fulfill God's promise through human means, we can fall into the trap of trying to earn God's favor through religious performance rather than relying on his timing.
2. The pattern of faith: Abraham's faith, credited as righteousness, remains the model for all believers. We are justified not by works of law but by faith in God's promise fulfilled in Messiah.
3. The continuing value of Torah: While the Torah is not the means of justification, it remains "holy, righteous, and good" (Rom. 7:12), revealing God's character and will for his people.
4. The unity of God's plan: The contrast between Law and Promise is not an opposition between two conflicting divine initiatives but rather a distinction between two aspects of God's unified redemptive plan.

By understanding Paul's allegory in its proper context, we can avoid the false dichotomies that have often characterized Christian approaches to the Law. We need not choose between faith and obedience, between Messiah and Torah. Rather, we can embrace the Torah as a gift from God, approached through faith in Messiah and fulfilled through the power of the Spirit.

Our exploration of the Sarah-Hagar allegory has laid the groundwork for understanding the proper relationship between Law and Promise in Paul's theology. The allegory, properly interpreted, does not pit the Torah against the Promise but rather contrasts two approaches to God's covenant: human effort versus divine fulfillment, works versus faith, flesh versus Spirit.

In the next chapter, we will build on this foundation to articulate a comprehensive understanding of the Law's purpose in relation to the Promise. We will see that far from being opposed to one another, Law and Promise serve complementary roles in God's redemptive plan, each fulfilling its divinely ordained purpose in bringing about the salvation and sanctification of God's people.

CHAPTER 6

A COMPLETELY SEPARATE PURPOSE

Thus far, we have examined the traditional interpretations that have dominated Christian theological discourse for centuries, questioned the premise that being "under the law" means Torah observance, explored the nuanced roles of the Torah as guardian and manager, and revisited the Sarah-Hagar allegory within its proper Genesis context. Now, we arrive at the culmination of our examination: the distinct yet complementary purposes of Torah and Promise in God's redemptive economy.

The Central Question Answered

Paul's direct question in Galatians 3:21 encapsulates the theological tension we have been addressing: "Is the Law then contrary to the promises of God?" His immediate and emphatic response— "Far from it!" (μὴ γένοιτο)—serves as a theological anchor and lynchpin. This strong negation, which could be rendered "Absolutely not!" or perhaps more popularly "May it never be!" in contemporary English, reveals Paul's insistence that we avoid perceiving an antagonistic relationship between Torah and Promise. Indeed, the apostle categorically rejects any notion that these two divine provisions stand in opposition to one another. Instead, they operate within their own distinct spheres in God's comprehensive plan of redemption.

The traditional interpretation of Galatians has often framed the relationship between Law and Promise in adversarial terms, suggesting that the former has been superseded or nullified by the latter. This view essentially suggests that the Torah functioned merely as a temporary measure—a stopgap arrangement, if you will—until the advent of Messiah, at which point it ceased to have continuing relevance for believers. Such a perspective, however, fails to account for the nuanced way in which Paul describes the role of the Torah and its ongoing significance in the life of faith.

It has been my contention, therefore, that a more faithful reading of Paul's argument reveals that the Law and Promise operate in different spheres with complementary purposes. They are not competing alternatives but rather integral components of God's unified redemptive plan. As such, it is not Torah observance that Paul so vehemently opposes in Galatians, but rather, Torah observance in a ritualistic and mechanical fashion. That is, a sort of Torah-as-religion, which seeks to utilize the Torah as a means of obtaining salvation.

The Promise, centered on God's covenant with Abraham and fulfilled in Messiah Yeshua, addresses the fundamental question of salvation and right standing before God. The Torah, conversely, was never intended to provide salvation but rather to serve multiple functions within the covenant community, including guiding believers in righteousness, revealing sin, and pointing toward the Messiah. Regarding Paul's "May it never be!" assertion to whether the Torah is opposed to the promise, Dunn writes the following: "The response indicates clearly that Paul would deny the very antithesis between law and promise which so many infer from verse 20. On the contrary, the role of the law is consistent with, integrated into that of the promise."[1]

The Purpose of Promise: Life and Salvation

The Promise, as Paul articulates it, originates in God's covenant with Abraham and finds its ultimate fulfillment in Messiah Yeshua.

---

[1] James D. G. Dunn, *The Epistle to the Galatians*, Black's New Testament Commentary (London: Continuum, 1993), 192.

This promise, which predates the giving of the Torah at Sinai by approximately 430 years (Gal. 3:17), established the foundational covenant relationship between God and his people. The essence of this covenant was God's declaration that he would bless Abraham and, through his seed, all nations of the earth (Gen. 12:3, 22:18). Paul identifies this promised "seed" as Messiah Yeshua (Gal. 3:16), through whom the blessing of Abraham comes to all who believe, whether Jew or Gentile.

The Promise, therefore, addresses the fundamental question of salvation and eternal life. As Paul states, "For if a law had been given that was able to impart life, then righteousness would indeed have been based on law. But the Scripture has confined everyone under sin, so that the promise by faith in Jesus Christ might be given to those who believe" (Gal. 3:21–22). Here, Paul explicitly identifies what the Promise provides that the Torah cannot: eternal life itself. The Promise, fulfilled in Messiah, imparts the divine life that enables humanity to enter into genuine relationship with God. This salvific purpose of the Promise is further emphasized in Galatians 3:13–14, where Paul writes: "Messiah redeemed us from the curse of the Law, having become a curse for us...in order that in Messiah Yeshua the blessing of Abraham would come to the Gentiles, so that we would receive the promise of the Spirit through faith." The redemptive work of Messiah liberates believers from the curse that accompanies Torah violations, enabling them to receive the promised Spirit. This reception of the Spirit, in turn, constitutes the evidence of adoption into God's family (Gal. 4:6–7), transforming believers from slaves to sons and daughters, heirs of the divine promise.

The Promise, therefore, addresses humanity's fundamental need for reconciliation with God. Through faith in Messiah Yeshua, believers receive justification (right standing before God), adoption into God's family, and the indwelling presence of the Holy Spirit. This transformation is not achieved through obedience to Torah commands but through trust in God's redemptive work in Messiah. As Paul reiterates throughout Galatians, this justification by faith follows the pattern established by Abraham, who "believed God, and it was credited to him as righteousness" (Gal. 3:6, citing Gen. 15:6).

The Promise, then, provides what the Torah never could and *was never designed to offer*: the spiritual life and relationship with God that sinful humanity so desperately requires. The Promise addresses the need for transformation from death to life, from alienation to adoption, from slavery to sonship. This is the exclusive domain of God's Promise fulfilled in Messiah Yeshua. Again, Dunn adds a helpful comment: "The point is, then, that it was not the law's function to 'make alive'; that is a power which only God can exercise. The implication is clear: to exalt the law, in effect, to the status of an angelic power, as though it could fulfil the divine role of making alive, is a mistake. That is not the role intended for the law by God—the passive of 'give' indicating God as the giver."[2]

The Multiple Purposes of Torah

If the Promise addresses humanity's need for salvation and life, what then is the purpose of the Torah? If the Torah is not intended to impart life, then why should we still strive to study it and obey it? Paul provides several complementary answers to this question throughout his letters, particularly in Galatians and Romans (as noted much earlier in the present volume). These various functions of the Torah reflect its multifaceted role in God's redemptive plan.[3]

---

2 Dunn, *Galatians*, 193.
3 I do not list these to be exhaustive, nor am I the first to create such a list. Ron Mosely has

1. The Torah as Revealer of Sin

One of the primary functions of the Torah is to reveal and define sin. As Paul states in Romans 3:20, "through the Law comes the knowledge of sin." The Torah provides God's standard of holiness, against which human behavior is measured, exposing the universal condition of sinfulness. Without the clear delineation of God's righteous requirements, humanity would remain ignorant of the full extent of its moral failure. Simply put, we learn what sin is, and its remedy, from the Torah, while Torah itself is not that remedy. This revelatory function is further elaborated in his letter to the Romans, where Paul writes, "I would not have come to know sin except through the Law; for I would not have known about coveting if the Law had not said, 'You shall not covet'" (Rom. 7:7). The Torah, by articulating God's moral standards, brings to consciousness the reality of sin that might otherwise remain unrecognized. It serves as a divine mirror that reflects humanity's true spiritual condition.

In Galatians 3:19, Paul addresses this function when he writes that the Law "was added on account of violations." The Torah made explicit what constituted transgression of God's will, thereby intensifying awareness of sin rather than providing a means of salvation from it. Commenting on this passage in his monumental exegetical commentary, F. F. Bruce states, "When Paul says that the law 'was added' (προσετέθη), he does not mean that it was added to the promise as a kind of supplement to it; he means that it was added to the human

---

a great list already produced, in which he lists nine different purposes of the Torah. I am merely narrowing the list down to the major different facets. Moseley's list, for instance, could have some of its own points consolidated such as the Torah's job of revealing sin as well as defining righteousness: by doing one, it does the other by default. Cf. Ron Moseley, *Yeshua: A Guide to the Real Jesus and the Original Church* (Baltimore, MD: Messianic Jewish Publishers, 1996), 44.

situation for a special purpose—a purpose totally different from that of the promise."[4] Once again we find a reinforcement of our central idea: the law is not opposed to the promise when it comes to the plan of God, only as a means of providing a path to God. While the Torah identifies sin, and prescribes a remedy, it is not the remedy itself. That is, while the Law tells us what sin is, it does not deal with sin on its own. This leads to the second purpose of the Torah.

2. The Torah as Guardian and Guide to Messiah

As we explored in Chapter 4, Paul employs three terms—παιδαγωγός (*paidagogos*), ἐπίτροπος (*epitropes*), and οἰκονόμος (*oikonomos*)—to describe the Torah's custodial role. This function involves guiding and preparing God's people for the coming of Messiah. Like a guardian entrusted with a child's care and education, the Torah supervised Israel during its spiritual childhood, drilling into them the principles and practices that would prepare them to recognize and receive the Messiah when he appeared.

This preparatory function includes both negative and positive aspects. Negatively, the Torah restrains sin through its prohibitions and penalties, functioning as a disciplinarian.[5] Positively, it educates God's people through its commands, narratives, and symbolic systems, shaping our understanding of holiness, sacrifice, covenant, and redemption. The sacrificial system, festivals, and ritual laws all served

---

4   F. F. Bruce, *The Epistle to the Galatians: A Commentary on the Greek Text*, New International Greek Testament Commentary (Grand Rapids, MI: W.B. Eerdmans Pub. Co., 1982), 176.

5   John Goldingay, *Do We Need the New Testament?: Letting the Old Testament Speak for Itself* (Downers Grove, IL: IVP Academic: An Imprint of InterVarsity Press, 2015), 63–64.

as "shadows of things to come" (Col. 2:17),[6] typological prefigurations that would find their fulfillment in Messiah Yeshua. In this way the Torah functioned as a tutor, leading Israel to recognize her need for a Savior and preparing her to understand the significance of Messiah's work when he appeared. So, it points out and defines sin, and it provides a map of sorts, signposts that point to the goal: Messiah.

3. The Torah as Guide for Sanctification

Beyond its role in revealing sin and pointing to Messiah, the Torah continues to serve as a guide for believers' sanctification. This ongoing function of Torah is often overlooked in traditional interpretations of Galatians, yet it is essential for understanding Paul's view of the Law's continuing relevance.

In Romans 7:12, Paul affirms that "the Law is holy, and the commandment is holy and righteous and good." The inherent goodness of the Torah stems from its divine origin and its reflection of God's character. As such, it provides invaluable guidance for those seeking to live in a manner pleasing to God. The Torah articulates the practical shape of love for God and neighbor, offering concrete expressions of these foundational commands. The classical "Golden Rule" given by Yeshua—"Treat people the same way you want them to treat you" (Luk. 6:31)—echoes, in a positive form, a teaching by Hillel from a generation prior: "'What is hateful to you, to your fellow don't do.' That's the entirety of the Torah; everything else is elaboration. So go, study."[7] In studying the Torah, we learn how to respond to God, but

---

6   For a complete treatment of Colossians 2, see R. L. Watson, *Let No One Judge You: A Pronomian Pocket Guide to Colossians 2* (Clover, SC: Pronomian Publishing, 2022).

7   Jacob Neusner, *The Babylonian Talmud: A Translation and Commentary*, vol. 2 (Peabody, MA: Hendrickson Publishers, 2011), 127.

also how we should view our fellow human beings, and how to orient ourselves towards both.

Moreover, Paul explicitly states that through the Spirit's empowerment, "the requirement of the Law might be fulfilled in us who do not walk according to the flesh but according to the Spirit" (Rom. 8:4). Far from suggesting that Torah observance is irrelevant for believers, Paul indicates that the Spirit enables genuine fulfillment of the Torah's righteous requirements. The issue is not whether the Torah remains a valid expression of God's will, but rather, *how* believers relate to it—and this is not as a means of justification, but as a guide for Spirit-led obedience. The "Law of Messiah" to which Paul so frequently refers, is just that: the Torah as observed and walked out in the Spirit-empowered life given by Yeshua.

This sanctifying function of Torah is further supported by Paul's statements, "Circumcision is nothing, and uncircumcision is nothing, but what matters is the keeping of the commandments of God" (1 Cor. 7:19). Similarly, in Romans, he writes, "Do we then nullify the Law through faith? May it never be! On the contrary, we establish the Law" (Rom. 3:31). These passages indicate that the practical, ethical guidance provided by the Torah remains relevant for believers' sanctification even still to this day. As Dunn says, "To be noted is the important corollary: that this is not a negative assessment of the law…simply an assertion that the role of the law is different from that of God or his Spirit. The law's proper role was already indicated clearly enough in 3:12—a role of directing life within the covenant, not the making alive by which God begins a new relationship (cf. Rom. 4:17) or completes it (cf. Rom. 8:11)."[8] To summarize his point, the purpose here

---

[8] James D. G. Dunn, *The Epistle to the Galatians*, Black's New Testament Commentary (London: Continuum, 1993), 193.

of the Torah is to direct what life in covenant community looks like. Yeshua summarized the commandments as "Love God...and love your neighbor as yourself" (Luke 10:27–28). These of course are passages taken directly from the Torah itself (cf. Deut. 6:5; Lev. 19:18), but the impact of the simplicity here should not be lost: obey the Torah because it guides you and orients your heart towards God, and obey the Torah because it guides you and orients your heart towards your fellow human. This does not merit justification: Yeshua has already done that.

Paul is not alone in affirming this ongoing role of Torah either. The author of Hebrews, discussing the new covenant, quotes Jeremiah 31:33: "I will put My laws into their minds, and I will write them on their hearts" (Heb. 8:10). This internalization of Torah, rather than its abolition, characterizes the new covenant relationship. Similarly, John defines sin as "lawlessness" (1 John 3:4), implying that Torah continues to provide the standard against which sin is measured. Throughout his letters Paul describes many different sinful behaviors, and arguably all of them are taken straight from the Torah.[9]

4. The Torah as a Blessing and Delight

Beyond these functional roles, the Torah is consistently presented in Scripture as a blessing and delight for God's people. "The law of the LORD is perfect, restoring the soul; the testimony of the LORD is sure, making wise the simple. The precepts of the LORD are right, rejoicing the heart; the commandment of the LORD is pure, enlightening the eyes" (Ps. 19:7–8). Similarly, Psalm 119 repeatedly expresses joy and delight in God's commandments: "I shall delight in Your statutes; I shall not forget Your word" (Ps. 119:16). A great and succinct

---

[9] Rom. 1:18–32; 1 Cor. 6:9–10; Gal. 5:19–21; Eph. 5:3–5; Col. 3:5–9; 1 Tim. 1:9–10.

quote on this comes from Bullock's textbook on the Psalms: "Thus the purpose of the Torah was to build a life lived in accordance with the will of God revealed in his laws, and to build a secure and safe community in which the Torah could be joyfully kept. [The Lord] has, therefore, provided a context of love (*hesed*) in which he gave his Torah, and those who keep it find that its benevolent purposes meet life's aspirations and produce human happiness."[10]

This positive perspective on Torah is not a view limited to the Hebrew Scriptures either. Yeshua himself affirmed, "Blessed are those who hear the word of God and observe it" (Luke 11:28). James refers to the Torah as "the perfect law, the law of liberty" (James 1:25), indicating that Torah observance, properly understood, is not burdensome but liberating. Likewise, Paul, commonly misrepresented as anti-Torah, confesses: "I joyfully concur with the law of God in the inner man" (Rom. 7:22). This expression of delight in God's Law belies any suggestion that Paul viewed the Torah as inherently problematic or burdensome. Rather, it accords with the consistent biblical perspective that the Torah is a divine gift, intended for the flourishing of God's people.

The Harmony of Law and Promise

Having delineated the distinct purposes of Torah and Promise, we can now appreciate their complementary roles within God's unified redemptive plan. The Law and Promise are not opposing forces of a fallen flesh and a risen spirit, but rather both are implements that God

---

10 C. Hassell Bullock, *Encountering the Book of Psalms: A Literary and Theological Introduction*, ed. Walter A. Elwell and Eugene H. Merrill, Second Edition, Encountering Biblical Studies (Grand Rapids, MI: Baker Academic: A Division of Baker Publishing Group, 2018), 220.

uses to work in harmony to accomplish his purposes for humanity. The Promise addresses what the Torah cannot provide: salvation and eternal life through Messiah Yeshua. The Torah, conversely, fulfills functions that the Promise does not directly address: it reveals sin, it guides believers in righteousness, and it provides a framework for covenant community. Together, the Torah and the Promise contribute to God's comprehensive provision for his people's redemption and sanctification.

Similarly, in Romans 3:31, Paul emphasizes that faith does not nullify the Torah but rather establishes it. The gospel does not render the Torah obsolete; rather, it fulfills the Torah's deepest intentions and enables believers to honor its righteous requirements through the power of the Holy Spirit (Rom. 8:4). This harmonious view resolves the apparent tension in Paul's teaching on the Law. On one hand, he emphatically rejects any attempt to achieve justification through Torah observance (Gal. 2:16, 3:11). On the other hand, he affirms the Torah's holiness, goodness, and ongoing relevance (Rom. 7:12, 7:22). These perspectives are not contradictory but complementary, addressing different aspects of the believers' relationship with Torah.

Implications for Contemporary Believers

This reexamination of the Law-Promise relationship has significant implications for contemporary believers, particularly regarding our understanding of Torah observance. If, as I have argued, the Torah continues to serve valid purposes in the life of faith—revealing sin, guiding sanctification, and providing a framework for covenant community—then believers today have reason to engage seriously with its commandments.

This does not mean adopting a legalistic approach that seeks justification through Torah observance. Such an approach would indeed contradict Paul's central message in Galatians. Rather, it involves recognizing the Torah as a divine gift that helps shape our understanding of God's character and will. It entails approaching the Torah not as a burden but as a blessing, a delight that guides our growth in godliness. This includes even the seemingly small (yet life-changing) practices like keeping Shabbat and festivals and refraining from eating things that are unclean.

Ultimately, the harmonious relationship between Law and Promise invites all believers, both Jewish and Gentile, to approach the Torah with reverence, humility, and joy. We recognize its limitations—it cannot provide salvation or spiritual life—while also appreciating its ongoing value as a guide for sanctification and a revelation of God's character and will.

Conclusion

In answer to Paul's pivotal question, "Is the Law then contrary to the promises of God?" (Gal. 3:21), we can confidently join him in declaring, "Far from it!" The Torah and the Promise, rather than standing in opposition, serve distinct yet complementary purposes within God's unified redemptive plan.

The Promise, fulfilled in Messiah Yeshua, addresses humanity's fundamental need for salvation and spiritual life. Through faith in Messiah, believers receive justification, adoption, and the indwelling Spirit—blessings that the Torah was never designed to provide. The Torah, conversely, serves multiple ongoing functions: revealing sin, guiding believers in righteousness, and providing a framework for covenant community. Both are divine gifts, integral to God's comprehensive provision for his people.

As we conclude this reexamination of Galatians, and the relationship between Law and Promise, may we approach the Torah not with suspicion or disdain, but with the same attitude expressed by the Psalmist: "Oh how I love Your law! It is my meditation all the day." (Ps. 119:97). And may we simultaneously rejoice in the Promise fulfilled in Messiah Yeshua, through whom we receive "the adoption as sons and daughters" (Gal. 4:5). For in this harmony of Law and Promise, we discover the fullness of God's provision for our redemption, sanctification, and eternal blessing.

APPENDIX A (POLOGETICS)
CRITICAL ENGAGEMENT

As noted in the Introduction, I wanted to the take the time to address a few arguments that are presented contra my thesis in this book, as well as some that are related to other passages found in the New Testament. Some of this I have already addressed in the material of the book itself, such as the quote from Schreiner regarding the temporary nature of the Torah, as addressed in Chapter 4. But three additional issues need to be taken up, I feel, to consider our view to be more holistic and not put ourselves in danger of merely proof texting our way through Galatians.

All Things to All People

In 1 Corinthians 9:19–23, Paul states that he has become all things to all people. He means this in the way he is willing to contextualize and present the Gospel, so that everyone can gain an understanding of the Gospel message (vs. 23). Here is the passage in question:

> To the Jews I became as a Jew, so that I might gain Jews; to those who are under the Law, I became as one under the Law, though not being under the Law myself, so that I might gain those who are under the Law; to those who are without the Law, I became as one without the Law, though not being without the law of God but under the law of Christ, so that I might gain those who are without the Law. To the weak I became weak, that I might gain the weak; I have become all things to all people, so that I may by all means save some.
> —1 Corinthians 9:20–22

Here Paul makes four statements: first, he became as a Jew; second, he became like one "under the Law"; third, he became like those "outside the law"; and fourth, he became weak. This is where the conventional view—that being "under the law" is synonymous with being Jewish—begins to break down. The phrase is superfluous at best (and deceptive at worst) if Paul is saying that being "under the law" means being a Jew. Not only that, but Paul was a Jew and had no qualms with calling himself one (cf. Rom. 11:1-2; Phil. 3:5; Acts 21:39; 22:3). However, an example of this conventional view can be found in the writings of the Puritan, Matthew Poole, in his Commentary on the Bible, which he wrote in the late 17th century:

> The Jews before Christ's death were *under the law*; many of them, though converted to the Christian religion after the death of Christ, apprehended themselves under the law, not as yet seeing the liberty with which Christ had made them free: saith the apostle, I, knowing the will of God, for a time, that the Jews should be indulged as to their weakness, *became as* one of them *under the law, that I might gain them*, that is, reconcile them to the Christian religion, and in some measure prepare them for the receiving the gospel.[1]

Poole is not the only one to reduce the passage down to a simple binary of Jew and non-Jew. John Calvin similarly boiled the passage down to a simple maxim: Paul lived like a Jew among Jews and a Gentile among Gentiles. He writes, "The particular instances are these—that among the Gentiles he lived as if he were a Gentile, and

---

1 Matthew Poole, *Annotations upon the Holy Bible*, vol. 3 (New York: Robert Carter and Brothers, 1853), 569.

among the Jews he acted as a Jew: that is, while among Jews he carefully observed the ceremonies of the law, he was no less careful not to give occasion of offence to the Gentiles by the observance of them."[2]

Now to be fair to the other side, I won't quote only sources which are four centuries or more outdated. Andrew David Naselli, writing within just the last decade (2020), states, "Paul strategically accommodates Jews—both those born as Jews and also those who choose to live as Jews under the Mosaic law. As a Christian, Paul (an ethnic Jew) is not under the Mosaic law, yet in certain situations he chooses to flex by following aspects of the Mosaic law (e.g., kosher rules, Sabbath regulations, circumcision) to gain a hearing to evangelize Jews (e.g., Acts 16:3; 21:20–26)."[3] Here the emphasis is on Paul's observance of Torah not as an ethical standard or moral obligation, but merely as a tool of outreach to Jewish people. This is the unifying thread that runs across the centuries of how this passage is interpreted. Hays adds some additional flavor to the conversation, suggesting thing "under the law" being referenced right after Jews could be referring to proselytes or even to God-fearers, a classification given to Gentiles who observed some parts of the Torah without undergoing full conversion.[4]

But are these assessments accurate? How do they relate to the analysis and alternative presented in the present volume? If we take "under the law" as being a shortened form of the phrase "under the

---

[2] John Calvin and John Pringle, *Commentaries on the Epistles of Paul the Apostle to the Corinthians*, vol. 1 (Bellingham, WA: Logos Bible Software, 2010), 305.

[3] Andrew David Naselli, "1 Corinthians," in *Romans–Galatians*, ESV Expository Commentary, ed. Iain M. Duguid, James M. Hamilton Jr., and Jay Sklar, vol. X (Wheaton, IL: Crossway, 2020), 300.

[4] Richard B. Hays, *First Corinthians*, Interpretation, a Bible Commentary for Teaching and Preaching (Louisville, KY: John Knox Press, 1997), 153–154.

curse of the law" then does that make it separate from "Jews" and from those "outside" the law?

To answer this, let's look at each phrase in turn. First, to become "as a Jew" does seem odd for the apostle who so openly recognizes his own Jewishness. But that is only the case if we assume he means "acted like" a Jew. Here, David Stern suggests helpfully what Paul's strategy was: "What he did was empathize with them. He put himself in their position (hence the lengthy phrase I use to translate 'became as'). He entered into their needs and aspirations, their strengths and weaknesses, their opportunities and constraints, their ideas and feelings and values—in short, to use the current vernacular, he tried to understand 'where they were coming from.'"[5] That is, he connected with them on their own level, on their own terms. He did this in order to win them over to the Gospel. Note that Paul offers no caveat; in the statements that follow, he will clarify that he himself is not "under the law" and that he is not "without the law" yet when it comes to his Jewishness, he offers no out: he does not deny being Jewish.

Second, he became as one "under the law." Once again, if we take this phrase to mean he worked to understand and communicate openly with those who sought to use the Torah as a means of justification, this passage then makes sense. Surely not all Jews (like himself and the other apostles) attempted to use the Torah for such a purpose, and as such, those "under the law" are not synonymous with Jews nor with Gentiles. Stern suggests the phrase to be a reference to Gentiles who had been Judaized by a specific sect, the same one causing trouble in

---

5 David H. Stern, *Jewish New Testament Commentary: A Companion Volume to the Jewish New Testament*, electronic ed. (Clarksville: Jewish New Testament Publications, 1996), 1 Cor 9:20a.

Galatia.[6] Stern also takes "under the law" to be a specific reference to legalism, and while I do not totally agree with each of his conclusions here, I do believe I align with him on the majority of his point. Thus, where "Jew" refers to Jews in general in 1 Corinthians 9:20, "under the law" refers to a subset that crosses ethnic boundaries: both Jews and Gentiles were susceptible to the "curse of the law" as he deals with in Galatians. As for himself though, Paul is clear: he is not "under the law."

Third, those "outside of the law" could be taken as a reference to Gentiles in general. In Romans 2, Paul writes that Gentiles, by nature, do not have the Torah. He uses the word ἄνομος (*anomos*), and the same word is used here in 1 Corinthians 9:21 to describe those "without the law." Paul once again offers the caveat: he is not without the law of God, and he is under the law of Messiah. Alternatively, this could be an instance where Paul uses language normally applied to Gentiles as an ethnic identifier to instead describe a set of people identified simply as "sinners." This is the approach taken by Wilber (following Stowers), who argues that Paul identifies this group simply as sinners (those who do not obey the law), and notes the correlation between Yeshua's own attitude of taking up communion with those viewed as sinners in calling them to repentance (Luke 5:27–32), with Paul's attitude of communing with sinners here in 1 Corinthians 9 as well.[7]

The fourth category, the "weak" ones, are themselves still a very controversial lot. I would suggest they are those who are part of the

---

6   Stern, *Jewish New Testament*, 1 Cor 9:20b.
7   David Wilber, "Following the Law of Moses in a Christlike Way: A Pronomian Reading of 'Law of Christ' in Galatians 6:2 and 1 Corinthians 9:21," in *A Disciple Named Timothy: Essays in Honor of Tim Hegg on his 75th Birthday*, ed. Rob Vanhoff and C.M. Hegg (University Place, WA: TorahResource, 2025), 207.

community already, but who do not have a firm foundation of faith. Paul uses the verb form of the same word in Romans 14:1–2, in reference to the one with a weak conscience (relating to foods of unknown origin), and in 1 Corinthians 8:9 where the "weak" are those who stumble over stumbling blocks, and in 1 Thessalonians 5:14, where he urges the congregation to help the weak. Once again, if we take "became as" to mean that Paul acted like them, one must ponder how the apostle of freedom would act like someone with weak faith. But again, following Stern, if we take the phrase to mean expressing empathy and understanding and communicating with the weak, the entire passage becomes much more coherent and palatable within the overall pericope of 1 Corinthians 9.

I believe that these, overall, are the best ways to understand these seemingly difficult phrases in this passage. The apostle was certainly willing to accommodate others, and without a doubt he was willing to go to great lengths to preach the Gospel however it needed to be heard. From Jerusalem to Mars Hill, Paul had no qualms with using whatever terminology or communication strategy necessary for the sake of the Gospel.

Days and Months and Seasons and Years

> You meticulously observe days and months and seasons and years. I fear for you, that perhaps I have labored over you in vain.
> —Galatians 4:10–11

These verses, like others we have addressed thus far, traditionally have been understood as referring to the Galatian observance of the Biblical calendar. Sabbaths and festival days seem to be in mind, and if we take the view that Paul is condemning Galatian Torah-keeping, then we have perhaps a compelling case that the referent in mind here is, in fact, the Biblical calendar and the feast days and Sabbaths. New Testament scholar Grant Osborne says this directly in his Galatians commentary, claiming, "these Galatians had started to follow the Jewish calendar and observe the Jewish feasts and the Sabbath laws."[8] Osborne is not alone in this perspective, either: Richard Longenecker finds a corollary between each of the four terms, with "days" referring to Sabbaths, "months" referring to new moon celebrations, "seasons" referring to pilgrimage and harvest feasts of Passover and Sukkot, and "years" referring to the Jubilee.[9] He does go on to note that he does not believe Paul has such specifics in mind, but rather in more general usage is likely using the four terms to refer to the whole gamut of Jewish calendar days.[10] Indeed, other scholars and commentators like Craig Keener, David DeSilva, and Jarvis Williams all largely conclude the same: Paul is saying the Galatians have erred at least in part because they have started observing the Sabbath and Holy Days.

However, as we have observed so far in the present work, things may not be so cut and dried. So, how then should we read Galatians 4:10–11?

First, we do so in light of the preceding context (as always). Paul just said in Galatians 4:9 that the Galatians were standing guilty of beginning to "turn back" to the elementary principles of the world that they had formerly worshiped. It bears pointing out that the Galatians were not themselves previously a largely Jewish group. That is,

---

8   Grant R. Osborne, *Galatians: Verse by Verse*, Osborne New Testament Commentaries (Bellingham, WA: Lexham Press, 2017), 133.
9   Richard N. Longenecker, *Galatians*, Word Biblical Commentary, vol. 41 (Dallas: Word, Incorporated, 1990), 182.
10 Ibid.

after all, part of why Paul is so upset here: some Jewish sectarians had come in and begun teaching a different Gospel. It was a new teaching, which the Galatians had not known. It makes little sense, then, that Paul would use the verb παρατηρέω in the present indicative for "observe" if it was something the Galatians were at risk of doing, as he addresses throughout the letter. Rather, the present indicative means they were already doing it (at least by the time it was reported to him). So then, whatever days and months and seasons and years they were observing has to fit contextually with the same elementary principles that Paul says they had turned back to. This is key to the verse itself, and part of why I do not believe it refers to the Biblical calendar's Sabbaths and feasts.

Now, at the risk of causing the reader to believe there is a monolithic scholarly consensus that indicates all scholars and theologians believe the so-called traditional view—that the "days" in question are Sabbath and feast days—let us briefly survey some additional views on this passage. Gary Burge, in his recent work *Galatians and Ephesians through Old Testament Eyes*, concedes that this passage could be referring to either-or: Roman or Jewish calendars, or possibly even "a mix of all the above."[11]

In his Galatians volume of the *Believers Church Bible Commentary*, George Rowland states, "The list of things being observed can easily make one think of the Jewish calendar, with its rituals and festivals. However, these terms are more general. They lack the greater precision of the list in Colossians 2:16—festival, new moon, and Sabbath."[12]

---

11 Gary M. Burge, *Galatians and Ephesians through Old Testament Eyes: A Background and Application Commentary*, ed. Andrew T. Le Peau and Seth M. Ehorn, First edition, Through Old Testament Eyes (Grand Rapids, MI: Kregel Academic, 2025), 111.

12 George R. Brunk III, *Galatians*, Believers Church Bible Commentary, ed. Loren L. Johns, Willard M. Swartley, and Douglas B. Miller (Harrisonburg, VA; Kitchener, ON: Herald

This point—at the risk of making an argument from silence—is actually a rather poignant one: Paul is clearly well-acquainted with the appropriate nomenclature for the Biblical calendar. Especially if he is speaking to those already beginning to observe the Sabbath and festival days, all the more we would expect him to use the same terminology he does in other letters when referring to the same thing. This, while not necessarily direct evidence itself, should be enough to give the reader cause for pause. But let us continue for now.

In his book *Galatians and the Imperial Cult*, Justin Hardin goes through a masterful examination of the issues with the traditional approach. He states, "In Gal 4.8–10, on the other hand, Paul rebukes his readers for observing days, months, seasons, and years, and explains that such practices were tantamount to worshipping the false gods from which they had been converted. If Paul was referring to the Jewish calendar, one is then at a loss to reconcile this unqualified statement with the evidence in 1 Corinthians (and Acts)."[13] The evidence from 1 Corinthians and Acts to which Hardin refers is that Paul does speak of certain festival days such as Passover and Unleavened Bread (1 Cor. 5:7–8), and Luke records Paul's journey to Troas as being at least temporally related to Unleavened Bread in Acts 20:6. Hardin goes on to give additional background information to explain why he believes the issue at hand is specifically that the Galatian believers were observing celebrations of the Imperial Cult of Rome, and that those were the days and months and seasons and years in question in Galatians 4:10.[14]

Press, 2015), 199.

13 Justin K. Hardin, *Galatians and the Imperial Cult: A Critical Analysis of the First-Century Social Context of Paul's Letter* (Tubingen: Mohr Siebeck, 2008), 121.

14 Ibid. 122–126.

We could surely go on to cite Troy Martin's 1995 journal article in which he emphatically states, "Interpreters usually cite the observance of the days, months, seasons, and years in Gal 4:10 as evidence for the Galatians' intention to live under law. However, this passage designates a pagan temporal scheme, not a Jewish one."[15] The rest of his article lays out his argument for why he can so confidently assert that the Jewish calendar is not in view here. Without belaboring the point too much, it remains that—even while a minority view—it is nonetheless still a viable one: that the days, months, seasons, and years in question are references to pagan observations rather than the Sabbath and festivals. Yet we must still ask the question: how does this fit into the overall letter? If the issue at the heart of Galatians is a misuse of the Torah, an attempt to use it to gain right standing before God rather than solely the justification provided by Messiah's death, burial, and resurrection, then why is a return to pagan celebrations even in view at all? This is certainly the most important question for the present passage, and the one that has driven most commentators to take the traditional view. So let's put the pieces together.

The issue in Galatia was one of outsiders coming in, trying to win converts, to get people away from Messiah by peddling a false Gospel. As can be seen throughout the letter, Paul is addressing a people in crisis, in particular a crisis of identity. Simply put, they did not know who or what they were: Jews? Gentiles? Something in between? Paul reminds them that in Messiah, they are heirs of Abraham (3:26–29). Paul offers them a stark warning about turning to an abuse and misuse of the Torah (as covered throughout the entirety of the present work)

---

15   Troy Martin, "Apostasy to paganism: the rhetorical stasis of the Galatian controversy," *Journal of Biblical Literature* 114, no. 3 (1995), 437+, Gale Literature Resource Center (accessed September 10, 2025).

but also a warning against turning back to paganism, or their "former ways" in which they were enslaved to things that were not gods (Gal. 4:9). Here one may take a cross-reference to 1 Corinthians 8:4–5 and 10:10, noting the likelihood that the reference to "things that were not gods" in Galatians 4:9 carries the same sentiment: they were enslaved not only to pagan idolatry but even to demons. The point here is that the congregation in Galatia was feeling spiritually homeless: not accepted by the mainstream strands of Pharisaic (and later Rabbinic) Judaism, yet also without special status in Roman society, and thus they were compelled to participate in the Imperial Cult. So the risk was two-fold: convert and become a recognized Jew and thereby be offered exemption from the Imperial Cult, or else return to the very pagan idolatry *of* the Imperial Cult.

Thus, Galatians 4:1–11 can be read in light of the identity struggle faced by the Galatian believers. This was a struggle not merely between Torah-keeping and grace, but between competing claims on the peoples' allegiance: a sectarian tradition, the Imperial Cult, and their newfound life in Messiah. The call is clear: true belonging is found not in ritual performance or ethnic heritage or cultural conformity, but in the transformative work of Messiah Yeshua. As Paul reminds the Galatians, the genuine fruit of the Spirit springs from a life rooted in him, not looking back to the structures that once held sway. For those of us today, our task remains: to anchor identity in Messiah alone, standing firm in the freedom that his kingdom brings, and refusing to trade our spiritual birthright for the false hope of systems that cannot save.

Torahism

Aside from addressing the challenging passage from 1 Corinthians 9, Galatians 4:10–11, and the other passages from Galatians already been dealt with herein, there remains one more source to be addressed before we can consider our apologetic work complete for our hermeneutical approach. This stems largely from one author who has taken it upon himself in recent years to challenge the very foundation of Messianic Jewish theology, and in particular, a pro-Torah hermeneutic. R. L. Solberg has gone to great lengths in his book, *Torahism*, to argue against the very core of the message that I present as the thesis of this work. He has coined the word "Torahism" to refer to the belief that followers of Yeshua should be keeping the Torah. Additionally, here only recently (less than a month prior to my own writing of this volume), he published a new work, *The Law, the Christ, the Promise,* which further promotes more of the same material. In the brief section below, I will seek to highlight some of Solberg's work and refute it. Note that I do not intend to rehash everything I have written thus far. In general, I believe the points presented in this book should stand on their own merit. On the other hand, I also do not want to feign ignorance of Solberg's own painstaking time in his work, nor do I want to avoid addressing a book so recently touching the very same topic and with such a similar title to my own.

In his opening to Galatians 3:15–29, Solberg writes the following:

> The Judaizers may have been trying to convince the Galatians that because the law came after Abraham, it supplanted the Abrahamic covenant. Paul says otherwise by way of an analogy. Once a man-made agreement has been accepted and signed by all parties, you cannot simply change the terms or declare it invalid without cause. How much more does God's covenant remain binding! Unlike the Sinai covenant, God's covenant with Abraham was unilateral. It was a one-sided agreement that required no reciprocal promise from Abraham.

In fact, when that covenant was cut, God put Abraham to sleep and established it by Himself (Gen. 15). It is a divine promise carried by Yahweh alone that does not depend on human actions or conditions.[16]

Solberg rightly points out the supremacy of the Abrahamic covenant over the Mosaic, and notes that the unilateral nature of the Abrahamic covenant is important because God alone participated while Abraham was asleep. He is also correct that the covenant is a divine promise, and that it does not depend on human action. Continuing, however, we begin to see an issue. He notes that the law was added (as Paul says in Gal. 3:19) because of transgressions. He then hinges his argument on the word "until" (the Greek preposition *achri*) and says "'until the Seed...had come' knocks the theological legs out from under any notion that the old covenant law was still in effect. That law came with an expiration date; it ended with Christ."[17] Solberg then gives a brief excurses on the purposes of the law, where he says the Torah served "at least three purposes. First, it was the terms of the covenant...Second, the law served as a national 'constitution' intended to form the Israelites into an organized nation...Third, the law was a written moral standard."[18] Solberg goes on to offer a word of caution

---

[16] R. L. Solberg, *The Law, the Christ, the Promise: A Verse-By-Verse Apologetics Bible Study through Galatians* (Grand Rapids, MI: Zondervan, 2025), 83.

[17] Ibid., 86. Solberg is not alone in his reference to the "expiration date" of the Torah. Matthew Harmon's commentary on Galatians uses the phrase as well. While Harmon does also note that the Torah's role is what is temporary, he nevertheless asserts that it was the Mosaic Law that is now ended in Messiah. Cf. Matthew S. Harmon, *Galatians*, Evangelical Biblical Theology Commentary, ed. T. Desmond Alexander, Thomas R. Schreiner, and Andreas J. Köstenberger (Bellingham, WA: Lexham Academic, 2021), 183.

[18] Ibid.

that he is not saying the moral injunctions of the Torah have been abrogated, yet he also offers no firm foundation for defending them.

In essence, Solberg's work—while recent—is not new. The same arguments have been presented time and again, many of which have already been addressed herein. While Solberg rightly indicates that the purpose to the giving of the Torah is multi-faceted—indeed, I myself point to at least 4 purposes in Chapter 6—he nevertheless undermines those purposes by suggesting that the Torah itself ends with the coming of Messiah. His emphatic statement cannot be summarized any more concisely or adequately than the direct quote above: the law was only supposed to be obeyed until the coming of Messiah.

How, then, could we (those in the Messianic or Messianic-adjacent spheres advocating for an unending observance of the Torah even to today) understand the Torah's "expiration date"? To address this—since I did not take this exact word to task earlier—let us examine the context. "Why the Law then? It was added on account of the violations, having been ordered through angels at the hand of a mediator, *until* the Seed would come to whom the promise had been made" (Gal. 3:19, emphasis mine). The word in question is indeed ἄχρις (*achris*), as Solberg noted. But what he misses is that, as I have argued, this is not a reference to the cessation of the Torah itself. We cannot take this one single word and use it as a lynchpin for the entire passage without considering the whole context. If we let Paul continue, he goes on to explain that it is not the Torah as a whole that ends with Messiah, but rather, the use and function of the guardian role of the Torah, in particular in its dealing with sin. That is why he notes that it was added "because of transgressions." Torah finds its terminal point (its goal) in Messiah Yeshua, who alone deals with transgression once and for all. In this way, the Torah provided a temporary means of dealing with transgression, which culminates in Yeshua, as illustrated by the tutor analogy. Like his contemporaries, including the Jewish authors of the apocryphal books of Wisdom of Solomon, 1 Baruch, and 2 Esdras, Paul expected the Torah to transcend time;[19] it is an eternal piece of the eternal covenant, much like the Sabbath ordinance of Exodus 31:12–17.

As we read through the end of Galatians 3 and throughout Galatians 4, Paul will continue to speak of the role of the guardian. At the risk of presenting an argument from silence, I could point out that Paul could have easily said the Torah ceased to function, or ceased to be observed, with the coming of Yeshua. However, he did not; he asserted that we are no longer slaves but heirs, no longer under law but under grace, no longer under a guardian. On this use of "until" here, Hegg notes that "the revelation of the Torah regarding how God provides redemption in the face of transgressions has its focal point in Yeshua. Once Yeshua had come and offered Himself as God's eternal sacrifice, the ultimate revelation to which the sacrifices pointed had been given. This is Paul's consistent perspective: the Torah leads to Yeshua (cf. Rom 10:4 and the continuing context of Gal 3)."[20]

While the "until" certainly does refer to the time of Yeshua's Kingship in our lives, it does not refer to the Torah's applicability to our lives, nor to our ongoing obligations as believers to obey God's righteous commandments. Rather, it refers to a specific *temporary function* that goes away when we arrive at our destination: Yeshua.

---

[19] Cf. 2 Esdras 9:37; Wisdom 18:4; 1 Baruch 4:1. These passages speak of the Torah as eternal. Isaiah 40:8 could also be referenced here, along with numerous sections from Psalm 119, Matthew 5:17-20, and Luke 16:17.

[20] Tim Hegg, *Paul's Epistle to the Galatians* (University Place, WA: Torah Resource, 2024), 256-257.

POSTSCRIPT

I hope and pray this book has helped you in your studies, and perhaps even in your struggles with some of the more difficult passages of Scripture. It is my belief that working through these passages produces some of the most powerful challenges and growth in our lives.

As for me, I continue to work on writing and publishing teachings and books (albeit somewhat slowly), both for the academy and outside of it. The best way to get in touch with me is by visiting my website: TorahApologetics.com.

—Jonathan A. Brown

BIBLIOGRAPHY

Arndt, William, Frederick W. Danker, and Walter Bauer. *A Greek-English Lexicon of the New Testament and Other Early Christian Literature*. 3rd ed. Chicago: University of Chicago Press, 2000.

Balz, Horst Robert, and Gerhard Schneider. *Exegetical Dictionary of the New Testament*. Grand Rapids, Mich.: Eerdmans, 1990.

Boles, Kenneth L. *Galatians & Ephesians*. The College Press NIV Commentary. Joplin, MO: College Press, 1993.

Bray, Gerald. "Review of Augustine's Commentary on Galatians: Introduction, Text, Translation and Notes by Eric Plumer." *The Churchman* 118, no. 1–4 (2004): 380.

Bruce, F. F. *The Epistle to the Galatians: A Commentary on the Greek Text*. New International Greek Testament Commentary. Grand Rapids, MI: W.B. Eerdmans Pub. Co., 1982.

Brunk, George R. III. *Galatians*. Believers Church Bible Commentary. Edited by Loren L. Johns, Willard M. Swartley, and Douglas B. Miller. Harrisonburg, VA; Kitchener, ON: Herald Press, 2015.

Bullock, C. Hassell. *Encountering the Book of Psalms: A Literary and Theological Introduction*. Edited by Walter A. Elwell and Eugene H. Merrill. Second Edition. Encountering Biblical Studies. Grand Rapids, MI: Baker Academic, 2018.

Burer, Michael H. *Galatians*. Edited by Tremper Longman III, Andreas J. Köstenberger, and Benjamin L. Gladd. Evangelical Exegetical Commentary. Bellingham, WA: Lexham Academic, 2024.

Burge, David K. "Jerusalem, City Of." In *Dictionary of Paul and His Letters: A Compendium of Contemporary Biblical Scholarship*, edited by Scot McKnight. Downers Grove, IL: IVP Academic, 2023.

Bibliography

Burge, Gary M. *Galatians and Ephesians through Old Testament Eyes: A Background and Application Commentary*. Edited by Andrew T. Le Peau and Seth M. Ehorn. First edition. Through Old Testament Eyes. Grand Rapids, MI: Kregel Academic, 2025.

Calvin, John, and John Pringle. *Commentaries on the Epistles of Paul the Apostle to the Corinthians*. Vol. 1. Bellingham, WA: Logos Bible Software, 2010.

Clarke, G. W. "Religio Licita." In *The Anchor Yale Bible Dictionary*, edited by David Noel Freedman. New York: Doubleday, 1992.

Cohen, Arthur A., and Paul Mendes-Flohr, eds. *20th Century Jewish Religious Thought: Original Essays on Critical Concepts, Movements, and Beliefs*. Philadelphia, PA: The Jewish Publication Society, 2009.

Cross, F. L., and Elizabeth A. Livingstone, eds. *The Oxford Dictionary of the Christian Church*. Oxford; New York: Oxford University Press, 2005.

Dunn, James D. G. *The Epistle to the Galatians*. Black's New Testament Commentary. London: Continuum, 1993.

Goldingay, John. *Do We Need the New Testament?: Letting the Old Testament Speak for Itself*. Downers Grove, IL: IVP Academic, 2015.

Haller, Hal M., Jr. "The Gospel according to Matthew." In *The Grace New Testament Commentary*, edited by Robert N. Wilkin. Denton, TX: Grace Evangelical Society, 2010.

Hardin, Justin K. *Galatians and the Imperial Cult: A Critical Analysis of the First-Century Social Context of Paul's Letter*. Tubingen: Mohr Siebeck, 2008.

Harmon, Matthew S. *Galatians*. Edited by T. Desmond Alexander, Thomas R. Schreiner, and Andreas J. Köstenberger. Evangelical Biblical Theology Commentary. Bellingham, WA: Lexham Academic, 2021.

Hays, Richard B. *First Corinthians.* Interpretation, a Bible Commentary for Teaching and Preaching. Louisville, KY: John Knox Press, 1997.

Hegg, Tim. *Paul's Epistle to the Galatians.* University Place, WA: Torah Resource, 2024.

Hübner, Hans. *Law in Paul's Thought.* London; New York: T&T Clark, 1984.

Johnston, Mark. *No Longer Slaves, but Sons: A Commentary on Galatians.* Welwyn Commentary Series. Welwyn Garden City, UK: Evangelical Press, 2018.

Keener, Craig S. *Galatians: A Commentary.* Grand Rapids, MI: Baker Academic, 2019.

Liddell, Henry George, Robert Scott, Henry Stuart Jones, and Roderick McKenzie. *A Greek-English Lexicon.* Oxford: Clarendon Press, 1996.

Lightfoot, Joseph Barber, ed. *St. Paul's Epistle to the Galatians. A Revised Text with Introduction, Notes, and Dissertations.* 4th ed. Classic Commentaries on the Greek New Testament. London: Macmillan and Co., 1874.

Longenecker, Richard N. *Galatians.* Vol. 41. Word Biblical Commentary. Dallas: Word, Incorporated, 1990.

Martin, Thomas W. "Hellenists." In *The Anchor Yale Bible Dictionary*, edited by David Noel Freedman. New York: Doubleday, 1992.

Martin, Troy. "Apostasy to paganism: the rhetorical stasis of the Galatian controversy." *Journal of Biblical Literature* 114, no. 3: 437+. Accessed September 10, 2025. Gale Literature Resource Center.

McKee, J. K. *Galatians for the Practical Messianic.* McKinney, TX: Outreach Israel, 2012.

McKenzie, G. Scott. *Walking Orderly, Keeping the Law: A Pronomian Pocket Guide to Acts 21:20–26.* Clover, SC: Pronomian Publishing, 2024.

Bibliography

Moseley, Ron. *Yeshua: A Guide to the Real Jesus and the Original Church.* Baltimore, MD: Messianic Jewish Publishers, 1996.

Naselli, Andrew David. "1 Corinthians." In *Romans–Galatians*, edited by Iain M. Duguid, James M. Hamilton Jr., and Jay Sklar. Vol. X. ESV Expository Commentary. Wheaton, IL: Crossway, 2020.

Neusner, Jacob. *The Babylonian Talmud: A Translation and Commentary.* Vol. 2. Peabody, MA: Hendrickson Publishers, 2011.

Osborne, Grant R. *Galatians: Verse by Verse.* Osborne New Testament Commentaries. Bellingham, WA: Lexham Press, 2017.

Poole, Matthew. *Annotations upon the Holy Bible.* Vol. 3. New York: Robert Carter and Brothers, 1853.

Rosner, Brian S. *Paul and the Law: Keeping the Commandments of God.* Edited by D. A. Carson. Vol. 31. New Studies in Biblical Theology. Downers Grove, IL: InterVarsity Press, 2013.

Ryken, Philip Graham. *Galatians.* Edited by Richard D. Phillips, Philip Graham Ryken, and Daniel M. Doriani. Reformed Expository Commentary. Phillipsburg, NJ: P&R Publishing, 2005.

Schreiner, Thomas R. *Galatians.* Zondervan Exegetical Commentary on the New Testament. Grand Rapids, MI: Zondervan, 2010.

Schreiner, Thomas R. *Paul, Apostle of God's Glory in Christ: A Pauline Theology.* Second Edition. Downers Grove, IL: IVP Academic, 2020.

Soards, Marion L., and Darrell J. Pursiful. *Galatians.* Edited by R. Alan Culpepper. Smyth & Helwys Bible Commentary. Macon, GA: Smyth & Helwys Publishing, Inc., 2015.

Solberg, R. L. *The Law, the Christ, the Promise: A Verse-By-Verse Apologetics Bible Study through Galatians.* Grand Rapids, MI: Zondervan, 2025.

Stern, David H. *Jewish New Testament Commentary: A Companion Volume to the Jewish New Testament.* Electronic ed. Clarksville: Jewish New Testament Publications, 1996.

Bibliography

Tellbe, Mikael. "Greco-Roman Religions and Philosophies." In *Jesus, the New Testament, and Christian Origins: Perspectives, Methods, Meanings*, edited by Dieter Mitternacht and Anders Runesson, translated by Rebecca Runesson and Noah Runesson. Grand Rapids, MI: William B. Eerdmans Publishing Company, 2021.

Tokajer, Eric D. *Galatians in Context*. Pensacola, FL: Eric Tokajer, 2019.

Waters, Guy Prentiss. "Ephesians." In *A Biblical-Theological Introduction to the New Testament: The Gospel Realized*, edited by Michael J. Kruger. Wheaton, IL: Crossway, 2016.

Watson, R. L. *Let No One Judge You: A Pronomian Pocket Guide to Colossians 2*. Clover, SC: Pronomian Publishing, 2022.

Wilber, David. "Following the Law of Moses in a Christlike Way: A Pronomian Reading of 'Law of Christ' in Galatians 6:2 and 1 Corinthians 9:21." In *A Disciple Named Timothy: Essays in Honor of Tim Hegg on his 75th Birthday*, edited by Rob Vanhoff and C.M. Hegg, 201–212. University Place, WA: TorahResource, 2025.

———. *How Jesus Fulfilled the Law: A Pronomian Pocket Guide to Matthew 5:17–20*. Clover, SC: Pronomian Publishing, 2024.

Wilson, Todd. "Under Law in Galatians: A Pauline Theological Abbreviation." *Journal of Theological Studies* 56 (2005): 363.

Wright, N. T. *Galatians*. Edited by Stephen E. Fowl, Jennie Grillo, and Robert W. Wall. Commentaries for Christian Formation. Grand Rapids, MI: William B. Eerdmans Publishing Company, 2021.

Zerbe, Gordon. *Philippians*. Edited by Douglas B. Miller. Believers Church Bible Commentary. Harrisonburg, VA: Herald Press, 2016.

www.ingramcontent.com/pod-product-compliance
Lightning Source LLC
Chambersburg PA
CBHW060341050426
42449CB00011B/2806